Patrick Donahoe

The Charlestown convent

Its destruction by a mob

Patrick Donahoe

The Charlestown convent
Its destruction by a mob

ISBN/EAN: 9783741193477

Manufactured in Europe, USA, Canada, Australia, Japa

Cover: Foto ©ninafisch / pixelio.de

Manufactured and distributed by brebook publishing software (www.brebook.com)

Patrick Donahoe

The Charlestown convent

THE

CHARLESTOWN CONVENT;

ITS DESTRUCTION BY A MOB,

ON THE NIGHT OF AUGUST 11, 1834.

WITH

A HISTORY OF THE EXCITEMENT BEFORE THE BURNING, AND THE STRANGE AND EXAGGERATED REPORTS RELATING THERETO; THE FEELING OF REGRET AND INDIGNATION AFTERWARDS; THE PROCEEDINGS OF MEETINGS, AND EXPRESSIONS OF THE CONTEMPORARY PRESS.

THE TRIALS OF THE RIOTERS,

THE TESTIMONY, AND THE SPEECHES OF COUNSEL.

WITH

A REVIEW OF THE INCIDENTS, AND SKETCHES AND RECORD OF THE PRINCIPAL ACTORS;

And a Contemporary Appendix.

COMPILED FROM AUTHENTIC SOURCES.

BOSTON:
PUBLISHED BY PATRICK DONAHOE.
1870.

Entered, according to Act of Congress, in the year 1870, by
PATRICK DONAHOE,
In the Clerk's Office of the District Court of the District of Massachusetts.

INTRODUCTION.

THE substance of the matter of the subjoined pamphlet was printed in seven successive numbers of the Boston Commercial Bulletin, of January and February. There was a larger call for the earlier numbers of the series than could be supplied by the publishers; and the compiler has been frequently requested to reprint the account of the Convent Burning and the Convent Trials in a pamphlet, and he has complied with the call. Very large additions have been made to the Bulletin account, — in proceedings copied from the newspapers of the day, opinions of the press, and of distinguished gentlemen of that time, who gave expression to their feelings in regard to this singular and almost unprecedented outrage, speeches of the counsel upon both sides at the trials, &c. All extraneous matter has been excluded, the object of the pamphlet and its publisher being to give the history of the events, as copied mainly from the publications of the day, with additions copied from the mouths of persons who were sufferers and witnesses of the riotous proceedings at Charlestown on the 11th of August, 1834. No partisan publication is proposed, and the only endeavor has been to

"Nothing extenuate,
And set down naught in malice."

THE BURNING OF THE URSULINE CONVENT AT CHARLESTOWN.

CHAPTER I.

ASSUMED CAUSES OF THE OUTBREAK.—RUMORS AND PREJUDICES.

The burning of the Ursuline Convent and School, upon Mount Benedict, in that part of Charlestown which is now Somerville, on the night of August 11, 1834, has recently been alluded to in a public political meeting, and discussion has been created in relation to circumstances connected with that unfortunate and disgraceful event, and to some of the persons who were supposed to have been associated with this dire transaction. As the revival of the subject has produced some discussion, and the whole facts relating to this by-gone affair are entirely unknown to a large portion of our people of the present day, a brief story of the stirring events of the time, gathered principally from the publications then drawn forth, will not be unacceptable. There were, as those know who then lived among us, many concomitant circumstances which fed the fire of prejudice, and assisted the lack of knowledge, which finally led to the catastrophe; and there were also hundreds of excitable and ridiculous rumors, calculated to stir up the passions of the mob, which, ignorantly, maliciously, or in a spirit of reckless and unthinking boisterousness or sport, joined in the exciting proceedings of that memorable night.

The Ursuline Convent was situated on Mount Benedict, about three miles from Boston, and its ruins are to be seen at this day. The principal building was an edifice of brick, about eighty feet in length, and four stories high. Among the other buildings was a farm-house and cottage. The grounds were laid out beautifully, and the whole appearance was quiet and lovely.

Although the name of the institution was the Ursuline Convent, "Nunnery" was its popular designation. It was principally devoted to the education of young ladies, and was, in reality, a female seminary of the higher order, though it was also a "religious house." At the time of the burning, there were within its walls, as stated from authority, twelve nuns and fifty-seven female scholars, many of them of a very tender age, placed there by their friends, principally Protestants, for purposes of instruction only: there were also three female attendants.

There had been some ill feeling between the officials and servants of the Convent and some outsiders, of an indefinite character. It was stated that the Lady Superior was not upon good terms with the Selectmen of Charlestown; and there were in the neighborhood a large number of laborers engaged in brick-making, who were principally from New Hampshire, and who probably were possessed of some indefinite prejudices against "Papists and Convents." One of these men, who was a principal at the burning, had a personal fight with the porter of the institution, who was reported to have set his dog upon a young lady who was passing the grounds, and stopped to look at them.

There were a plenty of stories in circulation at the time, most of them made up from surmises, or for the sake of idle talk, which only went to fan the flame which burst out on the 11th of August. Some of these were derived from Miss Rebecca Theresa Reed, who had been an inmate of the Convent, for several months, in the years 1831–32. The reports of Miss Reed and her friends led to great prejudices against the institution, including the school, among those who knew nothing in relation to them. She published a book in 1835, entitled "Six Months in a Convent," to which came a reply, or "Answer to Six Months in a Convent," by the Lady Superior.

All these reports, rumors, and transactions, were, however, only preliminaries, or auxiliaries, to the catastrophe and conflagration. A rumor had been put in circulation, and, of course, obtained full credence among the enemies of the Convent, that a nun had been made way with in some mysterious manner, or was held in imprisonment in the "Convent dungeon;" and the excitement which followed these reports was intense, and exceedingly magnified by circulation. At any rate the reports were noticed in many of the Boston papers, and were brought to the attention of the Charlestown authorities. On the Friday preceding the Monday night of the conflagration, it was stated in one paper that great excitement prevailed at Charlestown in consequence of the mysterious disappearance of a young lady at the Convent, and the following was given as an accurate account of the circumstances, as far as the editor could ascertain them:—

"The young lady had been sent to the Nunnery to complete her education, and became so pleased with the place and its inmates as to be induced to take the black veil.". Then it was added, ".that she subsequently became dissatisfied, and made her escape from the institution; but was afterwards persuaded to return, being told that if she would continue but three weeks longer she would be honorably discharged." Further, it was stated "that, at the expiration of this renewed period, her friends called for her, but she was not to be found."

It may naturally be supposed that such a statement would create a sensation, and it certainly had that effect; and, like everything of the kind, had its own good share of believers and disbelievers. The statement was made in the Mercantile Journal of the afternoon of August 8, and copied into the Morning Post the next day.

This report was also copied into the Boston Commercial Gazette, of August 9, accompanied by a declaration, given on the authority of Rev. Mr. Fenwick, then Bishop of the Diocese, that it was unfounded. It was added, that the Bishop would probably lay before the public the facts of the case on Monday, the 11th; in the mean time the editor stated, that the excitement was occasioned by the language of a Sister of the Convent, who was an invalid, and had been for some time deprived of her reason by brain fever. The same paper of Monday observed, that considerable excitement continued to exist notwithstanding what had been stated on the authority of Bishop Fenwick on Saturday; that the editor expected to be able to lay before the public the facts in the case, on the authority of the Bishop, but had since learned that he, understanding that a gentleman of Charlestown, residing near the Convent, and who was not a Catholic, having interested himself in the matter, and being satisfied that none of the remarks which occasioned the excitement were true, proposed to make a public statement. The Bishop had preferred to let the facts be given to the public by one who could not be accused of partiality, and had accordingly waited for that gentleman's statement.

But all the explanations were made too late; had they been prepared and published a day before, they might have averted the catastrophe. Perhaps they were in the operation of being put into type at the very time when the mob was surrounding the institution. Had they made their appearance twenty-four hours earlier, there probably would have never been any such regretful episode in the history of Massachusetts as "the burning of the Convent."

The first explanation was that of the Selectmen of Charlestown, and was as follows: —

To THE PUBLIC: Whereas, erroneous statements have appeared in the public papers, intimating that the liberty of a young lady was improperly and unlawfully restrained at the Convent in this town, and believing that said publications were intended to excite the public mind against that institution, and might result in unpleasant or serious consequences, the Selectmen, considering it their duty to endeavor to allay any such excitement, have, at the request of the government of the institution, fully examined into the circumstances of the case, and were conducted by the lady in question throughout the premises, and into every apartment of the place, the whole of which is in good order, and nothing appearing to them to be in the least objectionable; and they have the satisfaction to assure the public that there exists no cause of complaint on the part of said female, as she expresses herself to be entirely satisfied with her present situation, it being that of her own choice, and that she has no desire or wish to alter it.

     THOMAS HOOPER, SAMUEL POOR, ⎫
     ABIJAH MONROE, STEPHEN WILEY, ⎬ Selectmen.
              JOHN RUNEY, ⎭

CHARLESTOWN, August 11, 1834.

This note, it will be perceived, was not written in a style eloquent or perspicuous, but it conveyed information to the community, which should have been sought, ascertained, and set forth before.

The other statement, which appeared in the Morning Post, was that which was referred to by Bishop Fenwick as being about to be made by an impartial Protestant gentleman. It was furnished by Mr. Edward Cutter, a large brick manufacturer, and a man of much respectability, whose residence was not far from the Convent, and was in these terms :—

TO THE EDITOR OF THE BOSTON MORNING POST: Some excitement having been created in this vicinity, by misrepresentations that have come before the public, in relation to the disappearance of a young lady from the Nunnery in this place, I deem it proper for me to state certain facts that are in my possession respecting the affair.

On the afternoon of Monday, the 28th ult., the lady in question came to my house, appeared to be considerably agitated, and expressed her wish to be conveyed to the residence of an acquaintance in West Cambridge. I lent her my assistance; and on the succeeding day I called with the purpose of inquiring for the causes which induced her to leave the institution. I was informed that she had returned to the Nunnery in company with the Bishop, with a promise that she should be permitted to leave in two or three weeks, if it was her wish. Since that time various rumors have been in circulation calculated to excite the public mind, and to such an extent, as induced me to attempt to ascertain their foundation; accordingly, on Saturday, the 9th inst., I called at the Nunnery, and requested of the Superior an interview with the lady referred to. I obtained it; and was informed by her that she was at liberty to leave the institution at any time she chose. The same statement was also made by the Superior, who further remarked that, in the present state of public feeling, she would prefer to have her leave.

As it has been currently reported that the lady was not to be found, to allay the excitement in consequence of it, I have thought the above statement due to the public. EDWARD CUTTER.

CHARLESTOWN, August 11, 1834.

THE MOB AND CONFLAGRATION.

We have given above a notice of the principal moving causes which led to the destruction of the Convent. The rumors relating to them had increased, like the rolling snowball, until the day of the catastrophe. At that time it was observed that some of the reports of coercion and of violent management in the affairs of the institution had created among the people of the vicinity much irritation and excitement; but it was not believed that mob violence would be resorted to. They had increased, from day to day, however, until they threatened to burst forth in acts of outrage. It was understood that the publication of handbills, and an apparent movement among a certain class of the community, during the day which preceded the conflagration, produced among some observers a forcible impression that some great outrage would be perpetrated. Of this forewarning, however, no notice was taken by the civil authorities.

On the evening of the 11th, knots of half a dozen or a dozen men were seen, about half past eight o'clock, gathering in the neighborhood of the Nunnery. Soon after this a cart laden with tar barrels and other combustibles passed to the spot. This showed that burning was premeditated, and soon the work began. The doors and windows of the Nunnery were soon broken in by stones and other missiles, and a beacon fire was kindled, apparently as a signal to other rioters, upon the hill. The crowd quickly increased to a multitude. It was certain that this was a preconcerted movement; for the burning of the tar barrels was a signal for assembling, among the mass of citizens which would be collected, a large number who had entered into a combination for the destruction of the Convent.

A party of fifty to a hundred persons, or perhaps more, disguised by fantastic dresses and painted faces, after warning the inmates, who had all retired to rest, by wild noises and threats of violence, to make their escape, proceeded to make an active assault upon the house. The ladies of the institution, alarmed by these threats of violence, immediately took the children under their charge, and with them retired from the rear of the house to the garden, and made their escape to some of the neighboring dwellings. The assailants pressed the evacuation of the house with such haste, that it is said they laid violent hands upon the Lady Superior to hasten her movements. The distress and terror of the scene were heightened by the solicitude of the nuns for one of their number, who was confined to her bed of a disease which she was not expected to recover from. The assailants forced open the doors and windows of the Convent, carried most of the furniture, among which were three piano-fortes, a harp, and other musical instruments, into the yard, and there destroyed it. As they applied the torch, the fragments, as the flames spread through the building, were again thrown on to feed the fire. At about half past twelve o'clock they set fire to the building in the second story, and in a short time it was entirely destroyed.

A great number of persons were assembled at the spot, and were witnesses of the proceedings; and it was impossible to tell then, as it is now, why no measures were taken to repress them. It could not be learned that any magistrate or police officer came upon the ground. Several fire companies from Boston, Charlestown, and Cambridge repaired to the scene on the first alarm, and, when they ascertained the cause of it, a part of them returned home. A number of the fire companies, however, were present during the conflagration; and the effectual measures which were taken to suppress it appear to have been overcome by the great number of persons assembled, many of them evidently from a distance, for the apparent purpose of encouraging and aiding in the work of destruction.

Besides the Nunnery, several other buildings belonging to the establishment were also burned. The fire was deliberately communicated to the chapel, to the bishop's lodge, the stables, and the old nunnery — a large wooden building situated at a short distance from the others. The work of destruction was continued until daylight, when the mob dispersed. The pecuniary value of the property destroyed was not estimated at the time. It was from fifty to a hundred thousand dollars, and was insured, on building and furniture, for about sixteen thousand dollars.

The accounts further stated that the firemen of Charlestown looked on in silence, without attempting to extinguish the flames, and the Boston department were compelled by violence to abstain from all efforts to put out the fire or save the property. Everything was burned with the utmost deliberation, and without the slightest sentiment in opposition to the insanity of the mob. To crown the proceedings with an appropriate conclusion, the tomb at the foot of the gardens was entered, the coffins robbed of the plates bearing the names of the persons who lie buried there, and one of the coffins broken open, and its relics exposed. Even up to the next day there was not a single officer upon the spot to protect the remains of the dead from violation and insult.

It should be understood that all this is condensed from the newspapers which gave the first accounts of the rioting; and it is quite possible that some of the reports were exaggerated, though conversation with some of those who were present through curiosity, and endeavored to be witnesses of what was going on, gives proof that the Lord Abbott of Misrule himself presided over the frenzied proceedings.

A very large number of young fellows, less than twenty-one years of age, were mixed in with the mob, and joined in the proceedings, with all the recklessness of unrestrained youth when engaged in a "row" where there were none to withhold them. The religious character of the place was a special mark for their profane irreverence and ribald jests, and all sought to outdo each other in mad pranks and prurient specimens of blackguardism.

The Bishop had a library of religious books in one of the outbuildings; and Marvin Marcy, a young lad, son of the then keeper of a hotel, who was the very personification of fun and mischief, though juvenile in his appearance, with his sandy hair and almost girlish face, was a leader of a special mob of his own kind in their destruction. He took up the books, read their titles, or gave mock titles to them, and, acting as auctioneer, with all the readiness of an old hand at the business, made jeering remarks upon them and their contents, knocked them off, and tossed them into the flames. A stranger combination of materials was never gathered in a mob collection.

Most singular of all it was that this outrage was carried on so many hours of the evening and night, within so short a distance from Boston, and yet very little was known about it in the city. The firemen belonging to the few engines which went over the bridges did not return till late at night. The newspaper men appear to have learned nothing at all about the occurrence in their neighboring town; but there was not then the omniscient band of reporters in existence which is attached to the daily journals of the present day. There were more morning papers in Boston then than there are now, but not one of the conductors appears to have known of the proceedings. The Daily Advertiser had a postscript of five lines, in a portion of its edition of the next day, merely stating that the Charlestown Convent was burned the night before by a mob; and this casual and brief notice was all that the public gained the ensuing morning from the newspapers. It was before the days of " newspaper enterprise." At the same time there have been very few events in our city and neighborhood which have had such immediate and lasting effects.

The commotion among the Roman Catholics was immense. Proclamations were issued by the Governor of Massachusetts and the Mayor of Boston in regard to keeping the peace; the Charlestown Selectmen offered a large reward for the apprehension of the leaders of the riot, and the military was kept in arms in Boston, for some time, through fear of an outbreak. This was more than thirty-five years ago; and nothing similar to this sensation, either in character or dimensions, has since occurred among us.

The following account of the events is from The Jesuit, the organ of the Catholics of Boston at that time : —

DESTRUCTION OF THE CHARLESTOWN CONVENT.

It is our painful duty to record one of the most atrocious and disgraceful acts of violence ever perpetrated in any clime or civilized country. We allude to the destruction, by a lawless and fanatical mob, on last Monday night, of the magnificent Convent erected a few years since in Charlestown, by Bishop Fenwick of this city. This splendid institution had for its object the education of young ladies in all the branches of polite learning, and at the time of the woful disaster in question, had actually under the government of the Ursuline Ladies between fifty and sixty young ladies, chiefly of the best families of Massachusetts.

A report had been industriously circulated, for several weeks previous, that a young lady was detained in this Convent against her will; that she was immured in a dungeon, and there cruelly treated. However absurd the report, the fanatical preachers in Boston and the adjacent towns seemed glad of so favorable an opportunity to excite the public, and manifested every disposition to take all the advantage of it they could to asperse the Catholic religion, and decry its institutions. Inflammatory sermons were preached in the neighboring towns, and in one or two churches in Boston, particularly in the Baptist Church in Hanover Street, as we have been given to understand, with a view to rouse the people against Catholicity. Even Dr. Beecher could not forbear assailing it last Sunday, in three sermons, which he delivered in three different churches, availing himself of the opportunity which his return to this city afforded him of warning the public of the dangers of Popery, as evidenced by its general prosperity. Such violent fanatics are evidently the most dangerous of the enemies to good order, and to the peace and harmony of society.

However this may be, a small body of men were seen hovering about the Convent between eight and nine o'clock on Monday night. Shortly after, a car laden with tar barrels and combustibles passed on to the spot. These were soon set on fire as signals. The crowd then began to increase; shouts were uttered, accompanied with blasphemous speeches, and the most horrid yells and vilest imprecations. The doors and windows of the Convent were speedily broken in by stones and other missiles, when the mob rushed in, and in an instant began the work of destruction. The children were hastily taken out of bed and hurried out of the house; who all happily effected their escape, though half naked, to the neighboring houses. The nuns and Superior were the last to leave the dwelling. In a moment after, the entire building was in a blaze; but not before the most valuable articles in it, and which could be conveniently removed, were seized upon by the hand of ruffians that had entered it. The nuns saved nothing, not even a change of clothes. The tabernacle itself, with the holy altar, was rifled, the sacrament taken out of the blessed ciborium and thrown into the fields. A few pieces only of it were afterwards picked up and restored. From the house they proceeded to the sanctuary of the dead. At the bottom of the garden a beautiful tomb had been constructed, which contained the dead bodies of five or six nuns. These were torn out of their coffins and exposed. We shall make no comment on these proceedings; they speak sufficiently for themselves.

Early the following morning (the 12th inst.) the Bishop sent three carriages in quest of the nuns. They were found in different houses in the neighborhood. One of them was in a dying condition, being under a deep consumption at the time; another, in a state of mental derangement, reproduced by the noise and tumult attending on the dreadful occasion; all of them, in short, in a state of great debility, in consequence of the continual watching for several days previous. It was surprising to see, after so gross an outrage and so much suffering, the calm, the tranquillity which beamed upon their countenances, and their perfect resignation under the grievous calamity. Not a word of reproach, not a complaint was suffered to escape their lips. They undoubtedly felt (and who could not but feel!), for the act was base, was cowardly and cruel. From the houses in which they had taken shelter during the night, they were conducted to the house of the Sisters of Charity in Hamilton Street, in Boston, where they now are in a state of absolute destitution, subsisting solely on alms and the charity of their friends.

The amount of property lost by this execrable deed is exceedingly great. Twenty thousand dollars will scarcely restore even the building alone, which they have lost; and we may venture to assert, that the half of that sum will not replace the valuable furniture and costly instruments of music belonging to the Convent, and with which it was usefully adorned; for it is well known (and who knew it better than the intelligent and discerning citizens of Boston?), that no expense had been spared to render it one of the most splendid establishments of female education in this or any other country. The devotion of parents to it could not be excelled; their confidence in those to whom they had intrusted their children could nowhere be equalled. Notwithstanding all the alarms which fanaticism had excited during several weeks previous, and the menaces which had been continually uttered against the institution, not a single parent would withdraw his child from it. No; all of them, on the contrary, preferred to continue their children in it to the very last, at every hazard. They, too, have been great sufferers by this horrid act. Pianos of great value, belonging to several of the children, harps, guitars, gold watches, silver goblets and spoons, with all their clothing; these are among the losses which they have experienced. Some of them had been there for several years, and during this time had laid up a large provision of painting, of ornamental needlework, and of other beautiful specimens of their industry, with which they had hoped to charm and delight the eyes of their beloved parents, on their return home in a few months more; these also have been all destroyed, to the exceedingly great regret of these little ones, and to the no small disappointment of their friends.

Too much praise cannot be bestowed upon the excellent Mayor of Boston, and upon the city authorities generally, for their prompt, manly, and judicious arrangements in protecting Catholic property in this city, when menaced by the same infernal mob of incarnate devils, as soon as they began to manifest a disposition to renew in Boston the scenes which they had perpetrated in Charlestown. For, while they were suffered by the authorities in Charlestown (who assuredly should have lost no time in protecting, at least, what remained of the property of the unfortunate Convent) to continue, during the entire of the following day and night their depredations upon the fences, the fruit trees, the vines, even upon the dead in the tomb, and remaining walls of the once splendid building, without having taken a single precaution, or stationed a single municipal officer to interrupt such wanton destruction, the magistrates of Boston, to their honor be it spoken, were constantly upon the alert; and by the wise, prudent, and judicious measures which they at once adopted and vigorously acted upon, have gained the esteem and confidence of all their fellow-men, and elicited the loud approbation of every good and virtuous citizen.

We are happy to have it in our power to state, in conclusion, that there is but one opinion pervading the community at large in relation to this atrocious, diabolical deed, and in hurling upon it the detestation it deserves.

The Boston Evening Transcript, conducted by the late Lynde M. Walter, Esq., expressed the sentiments of the Protestant Church upon the outrage in the following terms: —

The general excitement, occasioned by the proceedings of night before last at Charlestown, and which yesterday, for the honor of the city be it said, raged among us with an earnestness corresponding to the atrocious character of that affair, has to-day, in a good degree, subsided. To the active exertions of the mayor, and other municipal authorities, the spirit and unanimity with which these were seconded by the whole community, and especially the great meeting called at Faneuil Hall, and finally, to the very commendable course pursued, as will be seen, by the Rev. Bishop Fenwick, must it be attributed, that after so stormy a day, the night passed off without disturbance in any direction. At Charlestown, also, the proceedings of the public meeting undoubtedly had a similar effect.

Among all the comment excited by this unprecedented enormity, we have noticed none which more justly describes the nature of the case than that of the Atlas, a portion of which is copied herewith.

"What a scene must this midnight conflagration have exhibited — lighting up the inflamed countenances of an infuriated mob of demons, ATTACKING A CONVENT OF WOMEN, A SEMINARY FOR THE INSTRUCTION OF YOUNG FEMALES, and turning them out of their beds, half naked in the hurry of their flight, and half dead with confusion and terror. And this drama, too, to be enacted on the very soil that afforded one of the earliest places of refuge to the Puritan fathers of New England, themselves flying from religious persecution in the Old World, that their descendants may wax strong and mighty, and in their turn be guilty of the same persecution in the New!

"We remember no parallel to this outrage in the whole course of history. Turn to the bloodiest incidents of the French Revolution, roll up the curtain that hangs before its most sanguinary scenes, and point us to its equal in unprovoked violence, in brutal outrage, in unthwarted iniquity. It is in vain that we search for it. In times of civil commotion and general excitement, of confusion, and cruelty, and blood; when the edifice of civil society was shaken to its base, and crumbling into ruin; when the foundations of the great deep were broken up, and rapine, and fire, and murder were sweeping like a torrent over the land; in times like these there was some palliation for violence and outrage, in the tremendously excited state of the public mind.

"But here there was no such palliation. The courts of justice were open to receive complaints of any improper confinement, or unauthorized coercion. The civil magistrates were, or ought to be, on the alert, to detect any illegal restraint, and bring its authors to the punishment they deserve. But nothing of the kind was detected. The whole matter was a cool, deliberate, systematized piece of brutality, unprovoked under the most provoking circumstances, totally unjustifiable, and visiting the citizens of the town, and most particularly its magistrates and civil officers, with indelible disgrace."

The violation of the tomb in the garden alone, would seem sufficient to justify these remarks, severe as they are. The feelings with which, yesterday morning, we witnessed the rude exposure of those remains to the glare of the day, and the gaze of an indiscriminate multitude, are such as we hope may never be aroused again.

EXCITEMENT IN BOSTON. — MEETING AT FANEUIL HALL, AND RESOLUTIONS THEREOF.

On the morning after the destruction of the Nunnery, as soon as the transactions of the previous night were known in the city, they produced a sentiment of regret and mortification at the outrage thus committed at midnight upon a family, or community, of defenceless females, and at the indelible stain inflicted on the character of the people. The Mayor, Hon. Theodore Lyman, Jr., promptly issued a notice, inviting the citizens to assemble at Faneuil Hall at one o'clock; and though there was but two hours' notice, "an immense multitude" assembled in obedience thereto, to take measures relative to the riot.

The subjoined account, taken from the Commercial Gazette, of August 13, will give a fair impression of the state of feeling in Boston : —

GREAT MEETING AT FANEUIL HALL.

One of the fullest and most animated meetings we ever witnessed, assembled yesterday at an hour's notice, in the Old Cradle of Liberty. The subject of mobs and mob law, always so exciting, we have hitherto read and heard of, it never having before come home so closely to the business and bosoms of every Bostonian. Charles P. Curtis, Esq., called the meeting to order, after having briefly stated that the unparalleled outrage which took place in Charlestown the night before was the occasion of it. Theodore Lyman, Jr., Esq., Mayor of the City, was unanimously called to the chair, and Zebedee Cook, Jr., appointed Secretary. Colonel Quincy now stated, that as President of the Common Council, he felt it incumbent on him, for, and in behalf of the people, to offer the resolutions, which will be found below, and which, after some very eloquent and pertinent remarks from the mover, and, after having undergone one or two amendments from other quarters, were unanimously adopted. Previous to this, however, the Hon. H. G. Otis rose to address the meeting, amidst the most deafening applause, which was more than once repeated, in the course of his most animated and eloquent remarks. It was pleasant, once again, to meet this splendid orator on the theatre of his youthful glory; and totally unprepared as he was, we must say, we have seldom, if ever, heard him to greater advantage. There was the same music 'in his voice, the same elegance in his gestures, the same beauty and felicity of expression, for which he has so long and so justly been conspicuous. The frost of age was on his brow, but the glow of youthful ardor was still predominant at his heart, and the thunders of applause, which made Old Faneuil ring again, were sufficient evidence that he still occupies the same high place in the affection of his fellow-citizens. It was, indeed, a cheering sight to see with what alacrity the people of all ages and descriptions came forth in the support of law and order, and for the suppression of a lawless and unprincipled mob; and we can have no doubt that the praiseworthy exertions of our excellent Mayor in this emergency will be met with a corresponding feeling on the part of his fellow-citizens.

Resolved, That in the opinion of the citizens of Boston, the late attack on the Ursuline Convent in Charlestown, occupied only by defenceless females, was a base and cowardly act, for which the perpetrators deserve the contempt and detestation of the community.

Resolved, That the destruction of property, and danger of life caused thereby, call loudly on all good citizens to express, individually and collectively, the abhorrence they feel of this high-handed violation of the laws.

Resolved, That we, the Protestant citizens of Boston, do pledge ourselves, collectively and individually, to unite with our Catholic brethren in protecting their persons, their property, and their civil and religious rights.

Resolved, That the Mayor and Aldermen be requested to take all measures, consistent with law, to carry the foregoing resolutions into effect, and as citizens, we tender our personal services to support the laws under the direction of the city authorities.

Resolved, That the Mayor be requested to nominate a committee of twenty-eight from the citizens at large, to investigate the proceedings of the last night, and to adopt every suitable mode of bringing the authors and abettors of this outrage to justice.

The following resolution was offered, on motion of John C. Park, Esq.

Resolved, That the Mayor be authorized and requested to offer a very liberal reward to any individual, who, in case of further excesses, will arrest and bring to punishment a leader in such outrages.

On motion of Mr. George Bond, the committee of twenty-eight were requested to consider the expediency of providing funds to repair the damage done to the Convent, and the property of its inmates.

The following persons compose the Committee proposed in the above resolution:—

H. G. Otis, John D. Williams, James T. Austin, Henry Lee, James Clark, Cyrus Alger, John Henshaw, Francis J. Oliver, Mark Healy, Charles G. Loring, C. G. Greene, Isaac Harris, Thomas H. Perkins, John Rayner, Henry Gassett, Daniel D. Brodhead, Noah Brooks, H. F. Baker, Z. Cook, Jr., George Darracott, Samuel Hubbard, Henry Farnum, Benj. F. Hallett, John K. Simpson, John Cotton, Benj. Rich, William Sturgis, C. P. Curtis.

CHARLESTOWN AND CAMBRIDGE.

In Charlestown, also, the town authorities promptly issued a notification for a meeting in the Town Hall, at three o'clock, for the purpose of obtaining an expression of opinions and feelings of the citizens at large "respecting the atrocious and unexampled acts of violence and arson perpetrated on the Convent on Monday night." The meeting was holden at three P. M., Dr. Thompson acting as chairman, and Mr. Dodge, the Town Clerk, as secretary. A committee, consisting of Hon. Edward Everett, Captain Whipple, John Soley, John Skinner, and William Austin, was appointed to draft resolutions declaring the opinion of the meeting. Rev. Mr. Byrne, who was appointed on the committee, declined to serve. The resolutions condemned the burning of the Convent in strong terms, and urged the establishment of a vigilance committee to secure the public peace.

The meeting also passed resolutions authorizing the vigilance committee to offer a reward of one thousand dollars for the detection of the projectors of the conflagration, and requesting the Governor of the Commonwealth also to offer a suitable reward. All the votes and resolutions were passed with unanimous and hearty expressions of approbation. Mr. Everett made some brief and energetic remarks upon presenting the resolutions, and Dr. Walker spoke at some length, and to the purpose, respecting the necessity of penetrating into the great conspiracy which must have preceded the execution of the diabolical plot. The Rev. Mr. Byrne made some just and practical remarks, and assured the meeting that he had used, and he hoped effectually, the most untiring exertions to prevent a reaction on the part of the Catholics, and the meeting listened to him with marked and approving attention.

A meeting was also held at Cambridge on the 13th, at which similar proceedings were had, and at which Judge Story, who was placed on the committee for this purpose, spoke at length in a solemn and impressive manner.

These meetings represented the sentiments of the great portion of the orderly citizens of Boston and vicinity at the time. There was a deal of excitement and much angry debate, — for the Convent had violent enemies, who could see nothing in the institution but a Nunnery, where women were imprisoned, with or without their will. The Irish Catholic population were terribly excited and enraged; they formed in groups in their sections of the city, and vengeance was feared, on both sides of the question, from the disturbed and angry feelings which were constantly elicited.

MEETING OF THE CATHOLICS. — ADDRESS BY BISHOP FENWICK.

The editor of the Gazette, in remarks following the report of the public proceedings, thus noticed the excitements of the day, and gave a sketch of the remarks of Bishop Fenwick to his people.

Fears were entertained yesterday that there would be fresh disturbances last evening. It was reported that the Irish laborers on the Worcester, Lowell, and Providence railroads were on their way to the city, in great numbers, for the purpose of aiding their Irish brethren in avenging the insult that was offered to them by the destruction of the Catholic seminary at Charlestown. It is true, we believe, that several hundred of these laborers arrived in the city last evening; but we have heard of no acts of violence on their part, or from any other quarter. The evening passed off quietly, at least so far as this city is concerned, although the streets were thronged until a late hour. We have rarely seen so many people abroad as there was last evening.

Much credit is due to Bishop Fenwick for the exertions he made to dissuade the Catholics from all acts of retaliatory violence. He despatched five or six priests in different directions, during the afternoon, to intercept the laborers, who were known to be on their way to Boston, and to instruct them not to raise a finger in defence of what they consider their violated rights. This was a judicious movement, considering the unparalleled state of excitement into which our citizens have been suddenly thrown by the outrageous conduct of a portion of the people of Cambridge and Charlestown.

We understand that all the Independent Light Infantry Companies were under arms last night, prepared with ball cartridges, to act in any emergency which might require their services. Hundreds of respectable citizens were also "on hand" to aid the civil and military authorities. Most sincerely do we hope that there may be no occasion for them to act.

So great was the excitement among the Catholics yesterday, that Bishop Fenwick deemed it necessary to call them together, in the afternoon, at the Church in Franklin Street. At six o'clock several hundred were assembled, when the Bishop came in and addressed them, for about thirty minutes, in a most eloquent and judicious manner. He deserves the warmest commendation from his Protestant fellow-citizens for the admirable style in which he managed this business. Previous to speaking, the Bishop read a part of the fifth chapter of Matthew, containing the following, among other verses: —

"You have heard that it hath been said, An eye for an eye, and a tooth for a tooth. But I say to you, not to resist evil: but if one strike thee on thy right cheek, turn to him also the other:

"And if a man will contend with thee in judgment, and take away thy coat, let go thy cloak also unto him. And whosoever will force thee one mile, go with him other two.

"You have heard that it hath been said, Thou shalt love thy neighbor, and hate thy enemy. But I say to you, Love your enemies, do good to them that hate you; and pray for them that persecute and calumniate you."

Bishop Fenwick then proceeded to address his hearers, embracing several hundred of both sexes. He spoke of the destruction of the Ursuline Convent and the adjacent buildings. He spoke also of the beauty and utility of that institution, and alluded to its growing popularity among the intelligent classes, both in this vicinity and at a distance. Among the pupils of the institution were some from Louisiana and the West India Islands. After denouncing the conduct of the incendiaries in appropriate terms, he asked, "What is to be done? Shall we say to our enemies, You have destroyed our buildings, and we will destroy yours? No, my brethren, this is not the religion of Jesus Christ; this is not in accordance with the spirit of that blessed religion we all profess. Turn not a finger in your own defence, and there are those around you who will see that justice is done you."

The Bishop then complimented the city authorities and others for the stand they had taken in defence of the rights of the Catholics; and he assured his hearers that they had the sympathies of all respectable citizens. The destruction of the Convent, he said, was an act of the most degraded of the human species, and it met with no favor from the intelligent people of Boston. He impressed upon the minds of his Catholic brethren the fact that it was not their duty to seek revenge for this vile act; and said that that man was an enemy to the religion he professed, and would put the Catholic church in jeopardy, who should raise a finger against their opponents at this time.

The Bishop said he had no fears that those who were present would act in opposition to his advice; and if any acts of violence were committed, it would be by those who, with perhaps a commendable ardor and alacrity, were rushing to their aid from a distance, and who may not have correct information on the subject. He enjoined it upon all present, as a solemn duty, to inform these individuals, if they should fall in with any of them, of what he had said, and the advice he had just given them.

He concluded his admirable remarks, which were delivered in a most impressive manner, by assuring his hearers that the public authorities were not idle spectators of what was passing. They are on the alert, said he, and it is your duty to remain quiet, to remain peaceable, and they will see you righted.

ALARM AND IRRITATION.

The pacific counsels and assurances, however, by no means restored confidence on either side. On the night after the conflagration a mob of rowdy men and boys, some of them reported to be armed with pistols and knives, paraded some of the Boston streets, menacing the Catholic Church in Franklin Street. About 11 o'clock they marched to the ruins of the Convent in Charlestown, where they completed the destruction of the garden, and made a bonfire of the fences that surrounded the premises, occupying the grounds till half past two o'clock on Wednesday morning, having, among other things, destroyed a number of valuable fruit trees, and torn up the grapery. There was no force, civil or military, to restrain their violence. The Charlestown military was on duty, however, the Light Infantry being specially posted at Mr. Cutter's house, having been sent there to guard his property, and they did not feel authorized to leave their station to go to the protection of the Convent. The mob was reported to have made a demonstration on the Charlestown Catholic Church, but finding it defended by the Warren Phalanx, they retreated without committing any actual violence.

The alarm increased in Boston, and the military were ordered out at night to protect the city. A popular alarm arose on Wednesday evening, which caused a good deal of excitement, occasioned by a report that the Catholic Bishop had communicated to some gentlemen who waited upon him, his apprehension that the Catholic population could not be restrained from some acts of violence in retaliation for the outrages which had been committed upon the property of their church. It was also reported that Catholics were arming, under the plea that they apprehended a further attack, and that an attempt was to be made to destroy their chapel in Charlestown. It was difficult to ascertain what foundation there was for these rumors, but they did much mischief. The people were told, through the press, that the civil authorities were taking all possible and suitable measures for preserving the public peace, and for acting, if necessary, in defence of it with promptness and vigor.

Some irritation also arose between Boston and Charlestown. On the 13th a handbill was issued in the latter locality, calling upon all good citizens to meet at Town Hall in the evening, which was signed "David Dodge, Town Clerk." The placard contained the assertion that "great and serious outrages had been committed there by *mobs from the city of Boston*, and other places in the vicinity." The statement was much resented by Bostonians, as the citizens knew very little of the troubles which had been going on for some time between the Charlestown people and government and the Convent authorities and servants. This attempt to fix the imputation of having furnished the mobs, by which the shameful outrages in Charlestown were committed, upon the city of Boston, and to screen the town of Charlestown from all shame in the matter, was not at all relished by the Boston people. The handbill stated that the mob was formed in Boston, — which was contrary to the known facts of the case. The charge was considered to be false and unneighborly, but it was one of the fruits of the excitement of the occasion, and the ill feeling was soon dissipated.

The publication by the Charlestown authorities was deeply resented by the Boston press at the time. The Charlestown Selectmen afterwards made an apology for the language used in the handbill.

All the young ladies of the Convent had property, such as pianos, guitars, harps, music books, silver cups, tumblers, spoons, thimbles, watches, chains, &c., and means were taken to procure the return of the articles. The Lady Superior, in an advertisement, mentioned the principal sufferers, and some of the losses were quite severe. Many precious mementos were missing. The plate of the Community, except what belonged to their place of worship, was marked in full. The Superior stated that nothing was saved; and the loss also comprehended money, to a very large amount, in gold, silver, and bank bills, the sum of which could not be strictly ascertained, as all the papers and account books were destroyed.

LETTERS OF SYMPATHY.

The Jesuit of August 23 in its further account of matters connected with the rioting, published a number of letters, which the editor said "were addressed to the Bishop immediately after the horrid outrage, and would show in what light this act of violence is viewed by the respectable portion of this community. They are selected from many others, merely as a sample of the general feeling of the better class of the community on this doleful occasion." Among those published were the following from Judge Story, communicating the proceedings at Cambridge, and from the President of the Massachusetts Senate.

CAMBRIDGE, August 13, 1834.

RIGHT REVEREND SIR: In behalf of the committee chosen by the inhabitants of Cambridge for this purpose, I have the honor to send you the enclosed resolutions. Nobody can feel, with more sensibility than the committee, the disgraceful nature of the outrage, which ended in the conflagration of the Ursuline Convent at Charlestown. We offer to you and the unhappy sufferers our sincere sympathy on this melancholy occasion; and we deeply regret, that in this land of religious liberty, proclaiming its duty to give all citizens and inhabitants an equal protection, a scene should have occurred so inconsistent with law, with justice, with humanity, and with religion.

In behalf of the committee, I have the honor to remain, Right Reverend Sir, your most obedient servant, JOSEPH STORY.

THE RIGHT REVEREND BISHOP FENWICK, D. D.

BOSTON, August 14, 1834.

TO THE REV. BISHOP FENWICK.

DEAR SIR: Although I have not the pleasure of a personal acquaintance with you, I cannot, as a citizen of this community, refrain from expressing to you the deep mortification I feel at the outrage committed on the Ursuline Convent, — an outrage scarcely exceeded in the history of crime.

I take the liberty of enclosing a check for a small sum, which I would respectfully ask you to appropriate at your discretion, in relieving any who may have been subjected to inconvenience, or suffering by this disgraceful proceeding. I remain, sir,
With sincere respect and esteem,
Your most obedient servant,
B. T. PICKMAN.

NO. 5 MOUNT VERNON PLACE.

The other letters printed were from David Lee Child, Esq., and from Dr. Henry B. C. Greene, a highly respected citizen, and a member of the Catholic church, who was absent at Saco, Me., at the time of the outrage.

On the Wednesday after the conflagration, Henry Creasy of Newburyport, a man about thirty-five years of age, committed suicide at the Bite Tavern by cutting his throat. Many rumors were circulated about the deceased, — that he had the communion chalice of the Convent in his possession, &c.; but it was only discovered that he had stated, just before he killed himself, that he had some of the sacramental wafer in his possession; and afterwards two pieces of the consecrated bread, which came from the chalice, were found in his pocket. This circumstance was the occasion of various publications in the journals of the day, and the statements respecting Creasy were the subject of much dispute and recrimination by the editors.

On the 15th of August, Governor John Davis issued a Proclamation, reciting the outrage, and calling upon all good citizens to aid in healing the wound which the laws had received, by the open contempt of their authority, and the wanton disregard of private rights. In the name of the Commonwealth he offered a reward of five hundred dollars for the detection and punishment of any person connected with the burning.

In the mean time, the city was in a state of constant uneasiness, from rumors of threats uttered by maddened Irishmen, that Boston and Charlestown would be laid in ashes. Whether such threats were made or not, is not known, but the reports were circulated, and many believed them. The Vigilance Committees of the two localities were in daily session, and the military were called out every night as a matter of precaution. The Light Infantry Companies of Boston mostly occupied Faneuil Hall, where their armories were then located, though some of them were on duty at the old State Arsenal in Pleasant Street.

The chartered military companies of that time were made up of the young men of the city with military tastes and inclinations, and they were separately composed of men of different classes and associations. The more aristocratic companies generally sympathized with the Catholic sufferers; the affinities of the companies more democratic in their opinion and conversation, were more with the rioters than against them. A gentleman who commanded one of the independent companies of Boston at the time, observed to the writer a few days ago, that the rank and file were altogether with the impulses which directed the mob. At the same time the men were perfectly subject to discipline, and were they called to perform duty, would be as efficient on one side as on the other.

On the Friday night after the burning a barn was set on fire in the vicinity of the Convent, and, with an adjoining house, was burned. Mr. Hayden, an American, occupied the latter, and two Irishmen were arrested for starting the flames.

The Committees of Vigilance kept their proceedings so quietly that little was known of them, but they had instituted sources of information; their standing offer of a large reward for testimony had its effect; they had many volunteers before them, and several arrests were made. At the close of the week eight men had been arrested, besides the two Irishmen charged with the late arson. Three men, Buzzell, Kelley, and Spear, had been committed for trial on the charge of burning, pillaging, &c. Spear was afterwards discharged.

The reports of the preliminary trials, which were holden at

Charlestown, as reported by the Boston papers, were exceedingly meagre and disconnected. Those who resided in Boston at that time, and remember the circumstances, understand that the utmost interest was taken in all these movements, and that there were so many present at all legal examinations that everything was immediately spread among those concerned as soon as information of it transpired, though very little got into the newspapers. The Vigilance Committees had set the example and enforced the necessity of secrecy in conducting the business ; and while the community knew about all that was going on, the newspapers apparently knew next to nothing.

The excitement among our people at the time was so great, that among the cautionary notices issued was one from the Mayor, requesting parents, masters, and guardians, during the then state of public feeling, to require all children and minors to remain at home after dark.

Captain Howard, of the revenue cutter Hamilton, stationed in Boston Harbor, brought his men ashore every night, during the first week of the excitement, and quartered them with the military at Faneuil Hall. They were well armed with cutlasses, blunderbusses, &c. The citizens formed clubs in the different city wards, and were out on patrol every night.

On the Sunday after the riot, a number of clergymen of Boston and Charlestown preached from texts appropriate to the events of the week. That of Bishop Fenwick, at the Church of the Holy Cross, was, "Father, forgive them ; for they know not what they do." Dr. Lyman Beecher preached a discourse on the subject from Rev. Mr. Blagden's pulpit at the North End.

The testimony, as published from the examining board at Charlestown, was not very luminous. The principal State's evidence was Henry Buck, who belonged in Claremont, N. H. ; had worked for Mr. Charles Adams, as a farmer, for a month and a half, and was present at the burning of the Convent on the night of the 11th. He was induced to attend, by hearing Mr. Adams state, on his return from Boston, that the Nunnery was to be attacked. He implicated Mr. Kelley as encouraging the mob, and furnishing fire from his house. Buck had been present at a previous meeting, and heard Kelley speak, and advise a postponement of the attack. Buck confessed his implication in all the proceedings. He was one of the first to enter the Convent, and broke in the doors with a piece of the fence. He saw the fires lighted, but did not assist in the incendiarism; but he took a small trunk as his share of the plunder, and secreted it in Mr. Adams's house. The motives of the rioters were various, as some were for plunder, and many merely went in for the excitement of the occasion.

Mr. Edward Cutter, who was a witness in the cases, made a long statement of his visit to the Nunnery, where the Lady Superior at first refused to admit him; but she subsequently attended him all over the building, from the cellar to the cupola, examining rooms, closets, and chests. He was certain that all was right; that no nun was forcibly detained; and he wrote a statement to that effect, and carried it to the office of the Boston Post for publication, the next day (Sunday), but was told that it would not be published till Tuesday; and before that the Convent was burned.

Prescott P. Pond, of Boston, the brother-in-law of Miss Reed, was examined before the justices at East Cambridge on the 19th. He was stated to be a volunteer member of engine No. 13, located in Leverett Street, and the examination ran largely upon the conduct of the members of that company at the Convent fire. The examination lasted two days, and Pond was committed without bail, as were William Mason, a member of engine company No. 4, of Charlestown, and William Young, Jr., of Woburn.

The case of a minor son of Colonel Roulstone, — a respected citizen of the west part of the city, — who was attached to engine No. 13, caused considerable interest. Captain Quinn, of the engine, was on the stand several hours, and the doings of his company were very closely examined into. Roulstone was discharged, and there was much rejoicing in old Ward V. on the occasion; flags were displayed, and there was a large gathering at the engine-house. It was announced, with some pride in the journals, that no member of the Boston fire department, and but one resident of the city, had been held for examination.

The excitement was continued some ten days or more, and the events were the most exciting which have been felt in Boston for half a century. Protestant gentlemen, who had daughters at the Convent school, were drawn into the controversy, and expressed themselves through the newspapers. The institution was temporarily removed to Roxbury, after the breaking up at Mount Benedict.

Of Miss Elizabeth Harrison, otherwise "Sister Mary John," the unconscious cause of all this loss, trouble, sensation, and disgrace, but little was known afterwards. Thomas Harrison, her brother, and Godfrey de Gilse, signing himself her "brother-in-law, and not a Catholic," made a public statement through the Transcript, about a week afterwards, in the form of a letter to the Superior of the Convent in relation to her. The substance was, that in an interview with them the day before, she stated that her health had been much impaired by the many and useless calls to see her at the Sisters' Institution. They were satisfied that she was perfectly contented, and would prefer death to leaving the community.

THE EXCITEMENT. — THE VIGILANCE COMMITTEE.

The foregoing rather brief summary of events, which were in the minds of a large majority of the people of Boston and its vicinity at the time, occupies the space of a week or more after the Convent was destroyed. Nevertheless, though the military companies were no longer on guard, and the volunteer and ward patrols were dismissed from service at night, the excitement could not be said to have entirely subsided for a long time after the occurrences which have been detailed. Indeed, we may say that the dregs of the excitement of 1834 still exist, and are liable to be stirred up at any time. There was a variety of sentiment in the community with regard to the proceedings, and the cause of them; some ignorance and much prejudice.

On the 20th of September, the Committee of Vigilance, appointed by the citizens at Faneuil Hall, made their report to the public, which was quite elaborate, went over the whole ground, argued the question from the standpoint of law, and order, and religious toleration, gave salutary advice, and suggested certain modifications of the law in regard to the duties of magistrates when a breach of the public peace is threatened. The committee admitted that the state of feeling in the community was anomalous; and in reference to the event, which was the occasion of their labors and investigations, they said, —

"It has come on us like the shock of an earthquake, and has disclosed a state of society and public sentiment of which we believe no man was before aware."

The committee declared, that the destruction of the Convent could be attributed principally to a widely-extended popular aversion, founded in the belief that the establishment was obnoxious to those imputations of cruelty, vice, and corruption, so generally credited of similar establishments in other countries, and was inconsistent with the principles of our national institutions, and in violation of the laws of the Commonwealth. The immediate cause came from the reports that one of the Sisterhood, Mrs. Mary John, formerly Miss Elizabeth Harrison, having fled from the Convent to escape its persecutions, and then been induced by the influence or threats of Bishop Fenwick to return, had been put to death, or secretly imprisoned, or removed, so that her friends could neither see nor obtain information concerning her. Such rumors were not only circulated in this city and vicinity, but extended to distant parts of the Commonwealth and other States. The report was signed by the late Hon. Charles G. Loring, its author, and chairman of the committee, and by thirty-seven members.

Notwithstanding the high character of the gentlemen who drew up the report, and its moderation of tone, the paper was severely criticized in some circles as being a whitewashing of the Convent. The story of Mrs. St. John, her fears, her flight, and return, were all detailed, and she was fully examined by the committee. She was a native of Philadelphia, and entered upon her novitiate twelve years before, in 1822.

CHAPTER II.

THE TRIAL OF JOHN R. BUZZELL.

THE Supreme Judicial Court of the Commonwealth met at East Cambridge, on the 10th of October, the day on which by arrangement of counsel, the Convent-burning prisoners were to be arraigned. John R. Buzzell, Prescott P. Pond, William Mason, Marvin Marcy (aged seventeen), Sargeant Blaisdell, Isaac Parker, and Alvah Kelley appeared, and pleaded not guilty. Five others, who had been indicted, had not been arrested. Their names were Nathaniel Budd, Jr., Benjamin Wilbur, Aaron Hadley, Ephraim G. Holwell, and Thomas Dillon.

The court named the 1st of December for the time of trial; but Attorney General Austin asked for a continuance until the April term, unless a special commission should be granted for an earlier trial. He spoke at length in defence of his motion, and mentioned the absence of a material witness as a reason for delay. G. F. Farley, of Groton, counsel for Buzzell, referred to the hardship of keeping men in prison six months without trial, and the other counsel for the defence spoke upon the same side. Mr. Austin alluded to the spirit which was abroad upon the subject. Many who were not bold enough to say the Convent ought to have been burned, were of opinion that a good thing had been done. They thought the parties had done evil that good might come. With this feeling, added to the right of the prisoners to object to twenty out of thirty-two of the jury, he asked if it was possible that a fair trial could be procured. Great difficulty had been experienced in procuring the attendance of witnesses, and the law was obliged to be put in force for this purpose.

Mr. Austin dwelt very seriously upon the state of the public mind — the fact that the crime had been committed in the presence of so many hundred people, who had calmly looked on. Those people were around now, and their state of feeling was the same. Acts of violence had been committed in the vicinity of the Court House; threatening placards had been posted up; anonymous letters had been sent round — he had received several of them himself. The jail had been surrounded by crowds who sympathized with the prisoners; an armed military force had been obliged to be kept up for its protection, and the officers who arrested the prisoners had been burned and hung in effigy. The speech of Mr. Austin was a remarkable effort even for that eminent attorney and counsellor; but it was also considered to be a singular exhibition of distrust of the juries which were to decide upon the cases, and of an offensive spirit towards the community in the whole neighborhood of the Convent, or of the greater portion of it.

Subsequently the Attorney General expressed a desire to have the trials in another locality. The court gave him the choice of having the trials in December or January; and he decided upon the former; and Chief Justice Shaw — the whole court agreeing — decided that the trials should commence on the 2d of December. Motions to admit prisoners to bail were refused. A lighter episode in the proceedings was the appearance of two women, named Emery and Hall, who were arraigned for contumaciously refusing to appear as witnesses. They were rather ignorant, and were very much frightened, and had been persuaded to stay away, but gave bail for their appearance as witnesses when wanted.

The trials commenced December 2. Attorney General Austin and District Attorney Ashael Huntington conducted the prosecution. Judges Putnam and Marcus Morton were on the bench with Chief Justice Shaw. Mr. Austin again presented his difficulties of being obliged to go into trial without material witnesses. He was not able to assign with certainty the cause of their absence, but supposed their non-appearance might be occasioned, in some degree, by a printed notification, which was extensively circulated, threatening with assassination all who should appear in court as witnesses against the persons who destroyed the Convent, "according to the oath that bound the parties together." Mr. Farley replied that the notice was quite as likely to be issued by persons hostile to the prisoners as by their friends. Mr. Austin withdrew his objection, and John R. Buzzell was placed on trial.

Forty jurors had previously been called, but many were challenged or set aside. In addition to the usual interrogatories, as to whether the jurors had conscientious scruples, had made up their minds, &c., Mr. Austin wished to ask them if they were under a prejudice that the testimony of a Catholic witness ought not to have the same weight as the testimony of a witness of any other persuasion? Mr. Farley objected. Mr. Austin said it would be perfect mockery to present the case, which must depend mainly on Catholic testimony, to a juror who had a bias and a prejudice against Catholics. The court decided that such a prejudice would not destroy the competency of a juror, and the question was ruled out. Another question was, whether a juror had said that he was glad the Convent was burned down, but was sorry it was done by a mob. The court decided against the relevancy of this question. The jury was empannelled, without further interruption, thus: William Farris, foreman; Abner Albee, Nathan Brooks, Joseph Bigelow, Artemas Carter, John Cutting, Perry Daniells, Osgood Dana, Thos. J. Elliott, Reuben Hayden, John Jones, William Rice. The indictment was read to the prisoners, and declared that they did, on the night of the 11th of August, burglariously and feloniously, enter, &c., the dwelling house of Mary Ann Ursula Moffatt, otherwise called Mary Edward St. George, and steal certain sums of money, and burn the building thereafter.

The Lady Superior, Madame St. George, was the first witness for the government. In explanation of her double name, she stated that when nuns assumed the veil, they also assumed a name different from that which they bore in the world. The lady wore a thick veil, which she declined to remove, until it was suggested by the court that this would be necessary in order to understand her testimony, when she unveiled. She certified to having received several communications relative to "the mysterious lady," Miss Harrison; that on the 10th of August one of the Charlestown Selectmen called and told her that the Convent would be destroyed if "the mysterious lady" could not be seen. She understood the lady designated to be Miss Harrison. On the 11th of August, five Selectmen came, and were conducted over the whole establishment. They remained three hours, and searched the building from the cellar to the highest apartment, looking through all the chambers and closets, and opening every box, even paint boxes. Two of the Sisters went with her to accompany the Selectmen, and one of them was "the mysterious lady," Miss Harrison. The Selectmen went away about three P. M., and at about nine she heard the noises come from the Medford road, "Down with the Convent! Down with the Convent!" She opened a window in the second story, and asked the mob what they wanted. They replied, that they wanted to see the nun that had run away. She went to fetch Miss Harrison, but found her lying in the arms of four Sisters, as she had fainted from fright.

After some parley the mob went off, saying they would return on Thursday and burn down the Convent; but they had not been gone long before they returned, and began to pull the rails from the fence to make a bonfire. They had previously fired a musket. Mr. Runey, a Selectman, came up with another person, and told her that he did not think he could quell the mob, but that if she and the inmates would throw themselves under his protection, he would do all he could for them. She replied, that if he wished to show himself friendly to her, to go and tell the people to desist from breaking the fences. He said he would do what he could, and passed on. The noise and riot increased. She notified the pupils that it was best for them to go to the summer-house; but before they could leave their dormitories the mob commenced breaking in the doors and windows. The remainder of the testimony of the Superior did not vary but little from the account which has been previously given of the destruction of the establishment. She referred to her loss of money; she had one thousand dollars locked in her desk, which was lost; and the whole loss she estimated at fifty thousand dollars of property in the institution. Some Spanish pupils lost considerable property in harps, jewelry, &c. The Superior was on the stand until the adjournment of the court. [The term "Mysterious Lady," was first used in a newspaper article in relation to Miss Harrison, and she was often alluded to in that manner.]

In her cross-examination, on the second day, the Superior stated that the nuns never called her "Divine Mother;" never confessed to her, but confessed to the Bishop. Miss Reed entered as a pupil to receive instructions, so as to be able to earn her living; she was taken in out of charity. She was not admitted to the school-room, as she was much older than the scholars. She desired to be taken into the community; and we promised that if she possessed sufficient strength of mind, courage and constancy, we might take her. She eloped about four months after she entered, because she was not allowed to take the white veil. She was not taken in as a candidate for the white veil. Candidates take the white veil in three months, and the black veil in two years and three months. Of Miss Harrison, the Superior stated, respecting her elopement from the Convent, that she had the brain fever — was out of her mind. She left the Convent July 28th, and before then she suffered much from the odor of the paint; was strange and extravagant in her manners, and said she was afraid she should lose her senses. She went to Mr. Cutter's house, and stopped there an hour, when Mr. Runey took her to Mr. Cotting's, at West Cambridge. The Superior admitted that in her conversation with Mr. Cutter, on the Saturday before the riot, when he said he was afraid the mob would burn down the Convent, she replied, that if they did, "the Right Reverend Bishop's influence over ten thousand brave Irishmen might lead to the destruction of his (Mr. C.'s) property, and that of others also." She considered that Mr. Cutter and Mr. Runey had acted unfriendly towards her in hurrying themselves so much in the affair of Miss Harrison.

Mary Ann Barker, otherwise Sister Benedict Joseph, was the next witness, and confirmed much that the Superior had stated. The Sister was a very beautiful lady, and her language and manner were those of a highly educated woman. She delivered her evidence with great clearness, and said the mob was very abusive towards the Lady Superior. They "called her a figure-head, and said she was made of brass."

Miss Elizabeth Harrison, or Mary St. John, the nun who left the Convent, testified that the cause was mental derangement, and that she had no trouble with the Superior. She was teacher of music in the establishment, and everything was done there to contribute to her happiness, and that of the other inmates. Her recollection of what took place after she temporarily left the community was very indistinct. Mr. Farley commenced to cross-examine her, when she suddenly covered her face with her handkerchief and burst into tears; and the prisoner's counsel, in consideration of what had been said respecting her health, refrained from asking more questions. She left the court under the escort of the Russian consul. Great curiosity was manifested to see the Convent ladies in the court-room.

When Bishop Fenwick was called, he objected to being obliged to place his hand on the Bible, as heretofore, when before the grand jury, he had only been asked to raise his hand. The court informed him that Catholics were usually sworn on the Evangelists, as it was believed they considered that form more obligatory than any other. The Bishop said he had no objection to take the oath in any way. He had only spoken, because he believed a stigma rested on Catholics in relation to this matter. It was supposed that a Catholic would not consider himself bound by an oath unless sworn on the Book. This was an error. The Catholic religion taught that an oath administered in any way, by a magistrate in a court of justice, was binding to the fullest extent. The court assented to his remarks, so far as they referred to intelligent persons like the Bishop, but with uninformed persons it might be different. Both in our courts and in England the course was pursued with reference to the religious belief of the witnesses, which seemed most likely to conduce to the attainment of truth.

The Bishop was then sworn, and took the stand. He went to Mr. Cotting's with Miss Harrison's brother, and found her in a state of derangement. His object was to take her to the Convent, clothe her well, and send her to her friends. He presumed she left the Convent because she was dissatisfied with her mode of treatment. Some days afterwards he proposed to send her home, but she begged and entreated to be allowed to remain. The property destroyed, exclusive of that of the pupils, he valued at from forty to fifty thousand dollars. It was his own. His cross-examination was mostly confined to religious matters. He said a bishop cannot be a Jesuit, but a priest may. The Catholic religion has never prohibited the use of the Bible, as a general rule. Members of the Catholic faith may have Bibles if they choose to purchase them; but we discourage them from reading any but our own. We do not consider the Protestant version a correct one.

Warren Dupee, a Boston fireman, was at the place on the night of the burning; but the Boston men could not work without the order of a Charlestown magistrate; and he saw no officer there, " not so much as a tipstaff."

Mr. Hooper, one of the Selectmen of Charlestown, testified to the good condition of the Convent.

Judge Fay, of Cambridge, and Levi Thaxter, of Watertown, both of whom had daughters in the institution, spoke highly of the manner in which it was conducted. They had both heard of the excitement, and drove out to the Convent on the night of the riot. They heard some conversation with individuals who occupied the gateway of the Convent, and the judge identified one of them as Buzzell. He was in his shirt sleeves, and was bespattered with clay, like a brick-maker. He was saying that he had " beat one Irishman, and was able to beat as many more as they could bring, three at a time." He used language which it was not proper to repeat in the court-room, as ladies were present; and the words were written down and handed to the court.

James Logan testified that he was present when the door was beaten in, and he entered with the mob. He saw no female. A number of lamps and candles were lighted. The first cry was to discover where the sick nun lay — to find if she was in the house. They searched, and gave up endeavoring to find her, and then began breaking the furniture. He saw them take things out of the drawers and put in their pockets, and then throw the furniture out of the window. They examined, till they were satisfied there was no woman in the house. He followed round with them. The first fire was set in the west end of the house, and the next in the east end. Saw Buzzell in the house, with a lamp in one hand and a trunk in the other, just before the fire was made, but did not see him build, or help build, a fire. Saw him break the furniture, like the others, with a club he carried in his hand. Saw him do it in different parts of the house. The reason witness went in was, that knowing there were helpless women and children there, and nobody to protect them, he went to assist them.

In cross-examination, Logan said he had never seen the prisoner before that night. To the question, "You are an Irishman?" he answered, "I suppose I am mixed in a little; came from Ireland, but not to America." Logan said he would answer no question unless the Attorney General told him to. He was one of three who first entered the building, and took two of the priests' vestments, and put them under his arm; also took some things and put in his pockets. The articles he carried from the Convent were worth, some people said, two or three hundred dollars. Among them were two silver canisters. He carried all to a friend's house, and went next morning and informed Mr. Byrne, the priest. He restored to the owners every article of the property. Mr. Austin objected to the question, "Have you a confessor?" and the court ruled it out. [Some other reports stated that Logan's friend informed Mr. Byrne about the property.] In answer to questions by Mr. Farley, Logan said, "I don't expect I ever testified before against the prisoner. Had never been called as a witness in relation to Buzzell before." Afterwards he said he had been to Concord, and was a witness there. [Before the grand jury.] He added, "I misunderstood the gentleman. I wish the jury to excuse me. I was subpœnaed to Concord, and examined there." *Question.* "Did you testify against Buzzell?" *Reply.* "If I testified he wan't in the building, I shan't answer you unless the Attorney General tells me to."

The witness was very choleric and crusty under cross-examination; and B. F. Hallett, who reported the trial for his paper, the Advocate, observed of him, "The cool impudence of this witness exceeded anything we ever saw on the stand." It was afterwards attempted to impeach his character.

Peter Rossiter, a servant at the Convent, had been beaten by Buzzell previous to the riot, but he did not know the reason for it. On cross-examination, he stated that the evening before his punishment two or three ladies were crossing the Convent grounds, to get on the turnpike road. The Superior told him to turn them back, to go out the way they came in, and he did so. Two got over the fence: one was not so spry, and he took her by the arm to talk to her. He did not set the dog upon her, as had been mentioned. He did not remember her calling for help.

On the third day of the trial, Fitch Cutter, of Charlestown, who lived near the Convent, stated that he recognized the voice of Buzzell among the rioters. He corroborated the evidence of Judge Fay.

Walter Balfour described what he saw of the events of the night. He lived in Charlestown, and his father was a minister of the gospel, though not settled. He went in to see if he could do any good. Went into the building with the mob; and, after they were in, their intention appeared to be to see if any persons were in the house, so that they might be got out. They examined the dormitories, rifled the drawers, and broke the furniture. When the fire was first set, he thought there were about a hundred and fifty individuals in the house. He thought that the whole of them — engine-men and all — were there for a bad purpose.

Dr. Thompson, of Charlestown, the attending physician of

the Convent, stated that he had previously to the riot attended an Irish servant of the institution for injury by blows from Buzzell. He also gave an account of Mrs. St. Henry, a nun lately deceased; her case was consumption, and he had no doubt her death was accelerated by the riot. He visited her the day previous, when she was in her usual health; he did not think she would ever recover, but thought she would live a year or more. She was a sister of the Superior.

The appearance on the witness stand of Henry Buck, who was one of the original conspirators, but who had turned informer, and was admitted as State's evidence, was the cause of some excitement in court. He worked with Mr. Adams, on Winter Hill, and knew that the destruction of the Convent was in contemplation some time before it took place. The rioters had two meetings at a neighboring school-house, about two weeks before the culmination. At their first meeting, only about twelve persons were present, who talked of sending out for assistance to burn the building that night. The same was proposed at the second meeting, but Alvah Kelley dissuaded them from it, proposing to wait three weeks, in order that "the mysterious lady" might be liberated. Buck's evidence was very direct against Buzzell. He saw the accused, as a leader of the rioters, on the night of the 11th, who told them to go ahead and burn the Convent; saw him break open doors, and throw out furniture. The first fire was in the chapel. He saw men stealing such valuables as they could put in their pockets. Buzzell interfered with engine-men who attempted to stop "a fellow" from setting fire to an outbuilding.

The cross-examination of Buck was long and searching, though not much was elicited therefrom. The object of the counsel of the defence was to show that he was utterly unworthy of credit. They brought out the fact that he had broken jail at Concord. Before the grand jury he stated his age at nineteen years, and he was evidently a third or fourth-class personage in social life. His testimony was not of so much value to the government as it was expected to be.

Colonel Elbridge Gerry, of Stoneham, who was present during the greater part of the proceedings on the night of the 11th of August, described them a little more methodically than most of the witnesses who were called to the stand were able to do. When he first reached the Convent, there were about sixty persons there. They had tried to lift the door from its hinges, but not succeeding, broke it to pieces. They had the usually adopted rules of organized associations; called "to order," and formed themselves into " a ring," that they might make arrangements for attacking the building. Some proposed to discontinue the attempt that night, as they were not properly organized. They thought they had not help enough to do the thing in a proper manner. Others swore that the institution should come down then, and proposed to make a bonfire with tar barrels, which would produce an alarm of fire, and bring a sufficient number of people together for them to go on with it. A tall man, and three or four others, went off, and returned soon afterwards with tar barrels, which they set on fire. Colonel Gerry said that he never saw the "tall man" before or since, until he saw him in this court-house at a preliminary examination. As far as he was capable of judging, the prisoner at the bar was the man.

Of the other witnesses examined, — and there were many of them, — little can be said, except that their testimony was confirmatory, or cumulative, as compared with the evidence of others. The case for the government was in readiness to be closed on the 5th; but in the absence of two witnesses, named Freeman and Miller, for whose appearance capiases were issued, the ground was surrendered to the defence.

Mr. Mann, of Lowell, a very eloquent advocate, opened the case for Buzzell on the morning of the 6th, and spoke full four hours. He was very impressive; was quite severe upon the prosecution and its witnesses; he evidently had the full sympathy of most of the large audience, and he dissected the evidence, and commented upon it, in a very effective manner. He said that the Lady Superior was brought into court entirely for effect, and he should be able to fully disprove her statements. Also, that Miss Harrison was not insane when she left the Convent; that she returned there for the mere purpose of saving the Superior's life; was to remain only three weeks, when her expenses were to be paid to her own home in Connecticut. She made the bargain, because she would not have upon her soul her broken vow and the blood of the Superior. He should also prove that the Superior had said to Mr. Cutter, in her interview with him, that "the Bishop had twenty thousand of the vilest Irishmen under his influence, who would tear down the houses of Cutter and others; and that the Selectmen might read the riot act till their throats were hoarse, and it would be of no use." In his declamation against the Catholic witnesses, Mr. Mann said that if the Bishop had twenty thousand Irishmen at his command, it was very easy for him to bring forward the three who had testified in the case. He should prove that Rossiter, the Irish domestic of the Convent, set his dog on some ladies who crossed the grounds; went up to one, who was not successful in escaping over the fence, threw her down, and gave her blows, of which she bore the marks for some days; that Buzzell afterwards met Rossiter, charged him with his unmanly conduct, and "then showed him how things of that kind were settled in this country." A subdued expression of applause throughout the court followed this. Buzzell, Mr. Mann said, was perfectly safe, if the testimony of Buck and of the Irishman Logan was not suffered to weigh against him. The counsel was very severe upon the latter, whom he accused of entering with the mob, and of stealing valuable articles, exclaiming, in conclusion, "And it was the testimony of this man — this *imported foreign* testimony — that was to cut Buzzell's throat!"

The address of Mr. Mann plainly indicated that the defence was to take wide grounds, and was not to be confined to the technical question of the innocence or guilt of the prisoner. It was also an impassioned reply to the fervid and denunciatory speech of the Attorney General, who had described the invasion of the Convent grounds, the expulsion, the fright, the midnight flitting, the mob outcries, the burning, and the whole wild and savage scenes attendant upon the affair, with all the thrilling and exciting eloquence, and the finest rhetoric of that distinguished lawyer and brilliant orator. Mr. Mann's speech was more popular in its tone, but was equally vigorous and forcible, and was bold and aggressive in its charges and replications. The audience appeared to be with him throughout, and drank in his words with an approving greediness which plainly marked the public sentiment, or that of a majority of the people present at the time. Very few more exciting speeches have ever been made in a court-room, and the friends of the prisoners took heart, as they followed him admiringly in his confident assertions, and nervous and animated style of delivery.

In the report of Mr. Mann's speech, it is stated that he alluded to the nature of the institution which had been destroyed, and said, "He did not come into court to abuse it, or 'its members; but the District Attorney having brought the character of the establishment into the case; having stated that it was instituted for charitable purposes, — for the benefit of the sick, the poor, and the needy, — it was important for the opposite counsel to follow up the investigation, and to show that these were not the objects. He should adduce testimony in regard to this point, and would now merely ask, whether, if the institution was such as it was said to be, fifteen thousand or twenty thousand citizens would have suffered a few individuals to destroy it? Where was our boasted militia? Where the Selectmen? They stand by with their arms folded, and suffer forty or fifty men, engaged in the transaction, to proceed unmolested. Must there not be some good cause for this supineness? Mr. Mann begged to be understood as not sanctioning the outrage. What he had said was merely for the purpose of showing that the Convent could not have been of such praiseworthy character as was described by the attorney for the prosecution.

"Then with regard to the Lady Superior. Mr. Mann could not conceive why that lady had been brought into court, except for the purpose of producing that effect which the testimony of a beautiful, highly-educated, and accomplished female would always produce. Her testimony was not wanted in the case; everything which she had stated, could have been as well stated by other persons. In connection with this subject — with this attempt to produce effect and excite sympathy — he would remark, that all the female witnesses, from the Lady Superior down to the domestics, appeared to be affected with colds, which they stated they caught on the night of the 11th of August. With every proper feeling of respect towards the Lady Superior, he must tell the jury that they were not to give any greater degree of consideration to the testimony of that witness than they would to that of the female Irish servant who had appeared on the stand. The life of his client was also at stake, and he trusted he should be held excused for saying that the counsel for the defence would call witnesses to impeach the veracity of the Lady Superior."

At the conclusion of Mr. Mann's address on the 6th, witnesses were sworn for the defence, and the first who were placed on the stand were introduced for the purpose of impeaching the character of Buck, the State's evidence, and the principal witness against Buzzell, which was pretty effectually done. Six witnesses were examined, some of whom had known him from childhood, and they declared him to be utterly unworthy of credit. Some had known him in New Hampshire by the name of William Henry Marsh, and one of them said that " no confidence was ever placed in anything that he said;" but as Buck had stolen a suit of clothes and ten dollars from him, he was supposed to be "prejudiced." Mr. Austin was a little nettled at this wholesale damage to the character of his witness, and asked one of his accusers if he was *intimate* with Buck. Mr. Farley objected to the question as an insult, and the Buck subject was dropped.

Much interest was taken in the next witness, Miss Rebecca Theresa Reed, the young lady of whom the Superior had said that she was taken in out of charity, and eloped because she was not permitted to take the white veil, for which she was not a candidate. She was described as " a delicate-looking creature," and her deportment on the stand was modest and pensive.

She said she was an Episcopalian; that she lived at the Ursuline Convent six months; was eighteen when she went there; was a choir sister, or a "choir religieuse," and was called Mary Agnes Theresa, which was her own choice of name. There were twelve recluse nuns there; the Superior was known by the name of Mamere, and it was the practice of the nuns to prostrate themselves before the Bishop.

This last style of evidence was objected to by the Attorney General and his colleague as irrelevant, and as having nothing to do with the case; and, at the suggestion of Judge Shaw, this part of the case was deferred, to give the court time to consider the admissibility of evidence upon the discipline of the institution.

One of the most revolting charges against the rioters was that of having shamefully desecrated the tomb in the grounds, and its relics; and Abijah Munroe, one of the Charlestown Selectmen, testified that on their visit to the Convent the day before its destruction, they were accompanied by Miss Harrison, in examining the tomb. Its padlock was so rusty that the key would not turn in it; he forced the lock, at the permission of Miss Harrison; but the hinges were in the same state, and they removed the door altogether. The tomb could not have been opened for a long time; and he remarked to the lady, in reference to the rumor that she had been secreted away, that she had not been imprisoned in the tomb, at all events. They replaced the door as well as they were able, but "a man might slue it round with a push of his foot." Another of the Selectmen testified to the same effect.

The court then adjourned to Monday, when the Chief Justice decided that neither party could go into the internal character of the institution; neither could the prisoner's counsel cross-examine a witness upon a matter irrelevant to the case, and afterwards introduce a witness to contradict this irrelevant matter thus drawn out. The judge went elaborately into the matter, in quoting authorities, &c., and his decision greatly disappointed many present, who wished to have all the inside arrangements of the Convent revealed to them.

Mr. Farley then proposed to prove that Miss Harrison was not insane when she left the Convent, which the court decided had no bearing on the case. Mr. Farley declared that the prosecuting attorneys had put this matter into the case. They had said the character of the Convent was good, had brought forward witnesses to prove this, and it was surely competent for the opposite counsel to go into these points. The whole matter hinged upon the derangement of Miss Harrison; and if it could be proved, as they were able to do, that Miss Harrison was not deranged, that would decide that the Superior, Miss Benedict, and Miss Harrison herself, had not testified truly. It was important that this matter should be correctly placed before the jury; and Mr. Farley was very earnest in presenting it to the court, but without effect.

After deliberation, the court decided that these matters should not have been brought into the case, either by the government or the defence; that everything relating to the internal arrangements of the institution was inadmissible.

Edward Cutter, who lived about a quarter of a mile from the Convent, testified that he never heard of any assemblies at the school-house, except at Buck's primary examination. He and his brother visited the Convent on the Saturday eve preceding the destruction, to make inquiries respecting Miss Harrison. The Superior said their inquiries were useless, and they should not see the nun. She accused him and Mr. Runey of intending to head a mob to destroy the Convent, which he denied; and she told him they might fetch on their mob, but that "the Bishop had twenty thousand of the vilest Irishmen under his control, who would tear down the houses of himself, his brother, Mr. Runey, and Mr. Kelley, and we might read the riot act till we were hoarse, without doing any good." She "steamed away" in that style for a considerable time, the witness said, till at last she brought in Miss John, and became quite good-natured. Mr. Cutter described his efforts to induce the nuns to go to his house on the night of the fire,— the children were already there. The Superior was much incensed with him after he took Miss John to West Cambridge; and that night she declared that he had delayed to make his statement in the papers on purpose to have the Convent attacked by the mob, and told him she wanted none of his assistance, and would not go into his house.

The counsel for the defence then brought in half a dozen witnesses to impeach the character of James Logan, the Irishman who saved the Bishop's vestments. It was testified that he was unworthy of belief, and that stolen property had been found in his possession. On Tuesday, Mr. Austin brought some witnesses to support Logan's character, among them Rev. Mr. Byrne, and Doctors Randall and Thompson, of Charlestown. Charges against him were explained away. Bishop Fenwick, and Daniel J. Coburn, who arrested Buzzell, were called upon some unimportant matters, when Mr. Farley stated to the court that the evidence for the prisoner had all been produced. There was some disapointment at the time, among the spectators and the public, that the internal arrangements of the Convent had not been more thoroughly ventilated. At the same time, it was universally admitted that Bishop Fenwick had conducted himself with great dignity, and with all proper courtesy, and most gentlemanly bearing through all the proceedings in which he had part, whether they related to court, jury, or counsel. The opinion was not so favorable in regard to the Lady Superior. There were a multitude of rumors constantly in circulation in Boston during the trial; and one morning it was currently, though incorrectly, reported throughout the city that Buzzell had committed suicide during the previous night.

Mr. Farley made the defence for the prisoner. He was a sound lawyer, and a gentleman who had considerable reputation in New Hampshire, legal and political, but he was not much known in Massachusetts. It was said that he left his home at New Ipswich, in his own State, because he so hated the rule of the Democratic party; while at the same time his first great work in Massachusetts was to defend one of the New Hampshire brickmakers, who, as politicians, were his everlasting opponents. He was a shrewd man, but was not gifted with extraordinary eloquence. He commenced by telling the jury to dismiss all the light matters connected with the trial from their minds; they were not now to decide a question of property; they were to declare whether the human being now before them should be cut off from existence — should be sent from the world, with all his imperfections on his head. He reviewed the evidence very skilfully; criticised sharply the government testimony, and insisted that the various charges against his client had not been substantiated before the court and jury.

Mr. Farley dwelt upon the rejection of Miss Reed's testimony, although evidence had been taken upon the government side with respect to the inmates of the Convent. He shook to pieces, as far as possible, the testimony of Buck and Logan, and he held up the character of his client as a son, husband, and father, which had never before been assailed.

The report says: " Mr. Farley adverted to the statute under which Buzzell had been indicted. He agreed with what his colleague, Mr. Mann, had said, as to the riot act being more applicable than any other act to such a transaction as the burning of the Convent; but that he did not mean to question the right of the prosecuting attorney to indict under the statute for arson. A mob, however, ought to be dealt with on the spot by the militia or *posse comitatus;* property would thus be saved, and the individuals engaged in it might be prevented from rushing headlong to destruction. If this was not done; but if, on the contrary, it was sought to punish after the crime had been committed, was there not danger that the innocent might be made to suffer with the guilty? The law made no distinction — would make none, when transactions of this kind were treated as the present had been. If a person went to such an assemblage as the one at Charlestown with the best intentions, and, under the excitement of the moment, countenanced or supported the rioters, he would be as guilty, in the eye of the law, as if he had been concerned in a conspiracy to effect the outrage. Degrees of guilt might exist; but under the present form of prosecution, the law could not take cognizance of them.

An innocent person might be arrested, and he could not tell his own story; he was only permitted to adduce such evidence as by the rules of law was admissible.

"With reference to the rejection of Miss Reed's testimony, Mr. Farley remarked that the government witnesses had testified that Miss Harrison was insane, and yet it never turned out that the counsel for the defence was not to call witnesses to rebut this testimony. Why the counsel for the defence had not objected at the time to the testimony adduced by the government, was because they did not consider such testimony improper; but should their omission in this particular prove detrimental to the prisoner, it would be a matter that they would never cease to regret during the remainder of their lives. * * * *

"Mr. Farley then concluded, by alluding to the fact that the prisoner had a wife and children, and an aged father and mother. The life of the most worthless member of the human family, he said, was precious; but the individual at the bar was a man of good character, and his life was valuable to others. If, however, the brother of the prisoner, now present, was to take the news to that prisoner's family that his life would be taken, such must be the case ; the consequences of the verdict of the jury the prisoner must suffer; but he (Mr. Farley) entreated the jury not to come to such a verdict until every reasonable doubt had been removed from their minds. He only asked them to do their duty ; to do to the prisoner 'even as they would that men should hereafter do unto them.'"

Attorney General Austin followed in reply, and in review of the whole case. He appeared to be personally, as well as professionally, interested in the case, inasmuch as the whole bias of his judgment was against the rioters. Those who have had opportunities to listen to his brilliant and caustic eloquence, to his energy and scope of declamation, to his fiery appeals and his capacious argument, may well understand how he acquitted himself in a case with which he had so far identified himself and his feelings, and in which, at the same time, he had fears of failure. His whole argument was full of force and eloquence. It was afterwards published in pamphlet form.

We copy some passages of the newspaper report describing the Convent and its inmates.

"I believe that this transaction unites within itself every circumstance of atrocity and brutality that ever met in any one case within the whole history of crime, — arson, robbery, sacrilege, *murder*, — and all perpetrated with the most shameless recklessness, the most brutal indifference, and the most fiend-like deliberation. Every excuse offered, too, in palliation of the act, does but dye in deeper guilt the miscreants who committed it. Let me ask you to go to the scene of this midnight destruction. Look at it before the torch of the incendiary had reduced it to a heap of ruins. You find a large estate, purchased and paid for by three native American citizens, held by titles of the same validity as those by which you, gentlemen of the jury, hold your farms and dwelling-houses. On this piece of land, formerly barren and uncultivated, a large pile of buildings is erected; the mechanics engaged in such erection, many of them neighbors of the institution, well and honestly paid. The grounds, which any but Vandals would have spared for their beauty, were laid out with regularity and taste. Lawns stretch away beneath the eye; gardens bloom around; and in one remote corner the hand of affection and piety had constructed the last sad sleeping-chamber of the hallowed dead. Within the walls, eight feeble women found their homes, with no protector but the God whom they served, and the laws they were willing to obey. This recluse society were religious women, devoting themselves to their Creator, under the protection of the boasted article in the Bill of Rights, which secures to every individual the privilege of worshipping God in any manner he pleases. But although retired from the world, they still had intercourse with it for its benefit, and were engaged in the most useful of all employments — the education of youth. They were a community of instructors and teachers. In a country boasting of the diffusion of knowledge within its limits, — the very existence of its institutions depends upon its people being educated, — those helpless females were devoting their little ability and strength to rear up the infant generation. And such was the confidence placed in them, that many of the children of your most respectable fellow-citizens were placed under their care: forty-seven of these children were under this roof at the time of the outrage. With no debt unpaid, or duty unperformed, giving no occasion of offence to any human being; unarmed, defenceless, because not apprised that they had anything to fear; surrounded by a population of a hundred thousand citizens, boasting their attachment to peace, tranquillity, and the law, those women retired to rest. Suddenly they are awakened by yells, hideous as those which startled our ancestors when the warwhoop of the Indian savage burst upon their midnight slumbers. They start up, frightened and alarmed, the terrified little ones gathering under the wing of their scarcely less terrified instructors. The bonfire, round which these semi-savages are dancing, throws its horrid glare in the rooms; stones, brickbats, and other missiles fly about the building; the windows and doors are driven in; life seems unsafe, and the inmates have to escape.

"They all do escape — all leave the place but one. One timid female only remains to face this ferocious mob; but the woman's heart, under the influence of nature, gains more than a lion's strength. Yes, gentlemen, the Mother, — not by the ties of consanguinity, — that old, infirm woman, whom you saw on the stand, she dares to remain, lest any of her children, any of her Sisters (by religion) should be exposed to the licentiousness of these lawless ruffians. She traverses the building from the basement to the cupola, opens every chamber, and runs from place to place, exclaiming in agony, like David of old, 'My child! my child!' But all, happily, are out of danger, and she goes back again to her own room, to save the little property of the institution. She finds it filled with armed men; she turns into the passage, and there beholds another band. She then retreats to the garden, where she finds the cowering children driven like doves from their dove-cot. All these leave the institution. Look at that sad procession, gentlemen, quitting the burial-place of their happiness. Mr.

Cutter has told you that when he first met them they did not speak a word; that they looked stupefied, and he had to gather them into a place of safety, as you would gather a drove of sheep into a pen. There was no weeping; no exclamations of sorrow; no tears — 'grief drank the offering ere it met the eye.' Presently the building is sacked; everything — the Word of God among the rest — is destroyed; fire is applied; that whole edifice is wrapped in flames, and rolls its accusing volume to the skies, till nought remains but heaps of blackened ruins. The children and Sisterhood are all fortunately preserved — all but one; she is killed by alarm and exposure. Do you not call this murder? What is murder but the felonious taking of life before the time allotted by Providence for its continuance shall have ceased?

"It would be enough, gentlemen, if the crisis attendant upon the work of destruction ended here. This, however, is but the beginning of the evil. The Commonwealth — the nation, is disgraced and degraded. We seem to be rolling back the tide of improvement, arresting the march of mind, and becoming more bigoted instead of more liberal. We proclaim toleration in our statutes, and are, in reality, less liberal than our ancestors when they persecuted the Baptists and Quakers. We talk of liberty, while we practise the most disgraceful despotism. We punish opinions and peculiar forms of worship, and are cowards as well as villains. We make war upon women and children, first inquiring whether there is a musket on the premises. The head magistrate of the town in which the outrage is committed — where was he? He goes up, looks round, admonishes the people that he thinks they have done enough; and then, having sore eyes, goes home and to bed. Where are the other magistrates, the militia, the neighbors? None are to be found. No neighbor, no magistrate, no friend, to take the part of these helpless women. It will be inscribed in our history, that here, at least, 'the age of chivalry is gone.'

"The mob enraged, luxuriated in riot to the extent of their wishes. And where did this take place? On the very hilltop where, not sixty years since, was consecrated, by the best blood in the country, an altar to liberty and the rights of man. Beside the very monument created to commemorate the patriotism of our ancestors, the man at the bar, and others, exhibited the baseness of their descendants; yes, left a mournful memento of the manner in which the freedom they had won had been erased by the race that followed them. The monument of Bunker Hill rises slowly; but the battlements are the work of a single night. Look to it, gentlemen, that it be not so with the State.

"Can any sympathy be felt for a man who makes war upon women and children? Where will be the pride of your American feelings when you take the stranger to Bunker's heights, and show him the slowly-rising monument, and your hearts beat warmly, and your bosoms expand at the recollection of the achievements of your fathers, which it is designed to commemorate; yes, where will be the pride of your American feelings when the stranger points to the other monument of ruins that towers so gloomily on the adjacent eminence? The chills of fifty winters would not send such an ice-bolt through your hearts. In Russia they enter baths heated to one hundred degrees of the thermometer, and then instantly plunge into the Neva; an American once tried this bath, and lost his life by the experiment; and the Convent rioters have prepared at Mount Benedict such a bath for American feeling. This crime is deserving of the severest punishment ever inflicted on the most flagitious offender; and to you, gentlemen, it is left to decide whether the prisoner was one of the perpetrators; and if you do come to a conclusion differing from mine, I must be content. But, good men and true, stand together, and hearken to the evidence.

"People who never saw each other before, are brought into this court to tell you that John Buzzell is one of the men. The cloud of witnesses never knew that they would be brought together here; nothing brings them here but the fact that they were at the scene. The trifling discrepancies of their testimony are proofs of its validity. It is truly laid down in the books, 'the usual character of human testimony is circumstantial *truth*, under circumstantial *variety*.' In proof of this principle, let us refer to the inscription affixed on the Cross, as it is given by the four Evangelists. St. Matthew says, 'This is Jesus, the King of the Jews;' St. Mark says, simply, 'The King of the Jews;' St. Luke says, 'This is the King of the Jews;' and St. John has it, 'Jesus of Nazareth, the King of the Jews.' Yet, notwithstanding these variations, who ever doubted that there was such an inscription?

"The counsel for the prisoner has drawn his scymitar across the neck of every witness for the government. According to him, there is not an honest man in the cause except the honest Iago at the bar. Yet among these witnesses is your own Judge of Probate, and gentlemen of similar character.

"We are told of the Lady Superior's threat of the twenty thousand Irishmen to Mr. Cutter. She undoubtedly did feel unpleasantly towards Mr. Cutter; he had done an unneighborly act when he assisted to carry away one of her family without letting her know it, and after creating the rumor which was published in the papers. It was natural for her to speak of retaliation, when Mr. Cutter spoke of the mob's tearing down the Convent; and if this cause be not settled right, I know not what may happen. But is Mr. Cutter's house pulled down? Have you seen, or do we see, anything of the twenty thousand Irishmen? Remember the Superior's deportment on the stand. Her property is destroyed and burned up; but does she show any heat, zeal, or malignity of heart? Nothing but the sublime spirit of her religion could have presented her in this court so mild, so calm, with such resignation as she displayed in the storm. * * * *

"The Ursuline Community are known throughout the world, and in history, as taking a part, an important part, in the active business of life, — the instruction of youth. When Napoleon and others suppressed convents in general, the Ursulines were spared, because they did not partake of the objectionable character attributed to other orders. * * * *

"The whole crime set forth in the indictment has been

proved; and if the prisoner is guilty at all, he is guilty of the whole crime. And I call upon you, gentlemen, to make no compromise with your oaths in this matter. We prove, by sixteen positive witnesses, that Buzzell was there. We trace him almost every moment of his time, from twilight to the next morning."

After analyzing and explaining the testimony, and vindicating the characters of the government witnesses from imputations cast upon them by the counsel for the defence, and complimenting very briefly Mr. Walter Balfour, Jr., as being the only true-hearted American that flew to the protection of the Convent, Mr. Austin terminated his argument by reiterating his assurance to the jury that the proceedings in the court must be revised by another authority before a single hair of Buzzell's head should be touched. He also took occasion to remark, that the counsel for the Commonwealth were under no obligations to the Selectmen of Charlestown for anything connected with any part of this or any other trial.

On the 10th and 11th, Chief Justice Shaw delivered the charge to the jury, and he explained to them the condition of Buzzell before them. His life was safe as regarded the charge of arson, as it had not been proved that any persons were in the buildings when they were set on fire. In respect to the second fatal charge of burglary, the Judge considered that Buzzell was differently circumstanced, as the law was thus: "If any person shall break into a house with felonious intent, armed with any dangerous weapon, or arming himself within, or shall assault any person lawfully in the house, he shall suffer death."

It was laid down by the court, that according to the statute of 1830, upon the crime of arson, if no person was *lawfully* in the Convent when it was set on fire, it did not amount to a capital offence, and was not punishable with death. [The Attorney General, in reference to that principle, called the attention of the court to the fact that Messrs. Balfour and Logan, who were in the building when fire was applied, were lawfully there.] But the court decided that they were not there lawfully, in the sense of the statute, though in other senses their presence there was both lawful and laudable, viz., to afford protection and assistance, if there were any persons in the Convent requiring them. Upon the point of burglary, it was laid down to be a capital offence to break into a dwelling-house, while there were persons lawfully in it, with a felonious intent, and armed with a dangerous weapon. Nor is it necessary to *prove* the intent, if the party be armed with a weapon competent to do the mischief, and does it. The court considered the testimony of the Superior, that she was in the Convent when the rioters made their forcible entry, corroborated by the other witnesses, and they therefore fell within the scope and effect of this principle. The court did not sustain the proposition advanced by the Attorney General, that the nuns, being in the summer-house, — a part of the curtilage of the dwellinghouse, — they were, in the eye of the law, in the dwellinghouse.

The jury were instructed that they would acquit or convict the prisoner upon all or either of the counts of the indictment; on those which were capital, or on those which were only punishable with confinement to hard labor in the State Prison.

The Chief Justice then entered generally upon the evidence of the cause, with the remark that the commission of the crime had been conceded, and the whole case was resolved into a question of identity; and the evidence upon this point he stated to the jury with great impartiality, and abstained scrupulously from all remarks or suggestions calculated in the remotest degree to interfere with the peculiar province of the jury to decide upon its effect and weight against the prisoner. Judge Shaw stated, that if Buzzell was the man identified by the first series of witnesses, yet after the bonfire, there was no evidence against him but that of Buck and Logan, who saw him in the Convent, with a club in his hand, doing mischief. As Logan's character for truth had been questioned, His Honor instructed the jury to regard principally the *intrinsic* probability of his statement, and its corroboration by other witnesses, and also the circumstance that he was not contradicted in one fact. A witness might be incompetent from infamy or interest; but a surmise by counsel against a witness ought not to have any bearing on the minds of the jury. It having been incidentally mentioned that stolen plants were once found in Logan's possession, His Honor charged the jury, out of justice to Logan, to disregard absolutely and entirely the remark, if they heard it, as Logan was not allowed to explain that circumstance, although he brought witnesses into court, upon very short notice, to testify upon that point. The rule of evidence that prevents him from introducing evidence upon any particular charge, is founded upon common-sense principles. A witness ought to have notice, if any such charge is to be brought against him, that he may have opportunity to bring testimony to rebut it, which would lead us into a host of collateral trials, during the pendency of the main one, to the entire obstruction of the regular course of justice.

It had been contended that the evidence introduced to support Logan's character for truth against those witnesses who impeach it, was merely *negative;* but when witnesses, knowing a party, swear that they know nothing against his character, though that be negative in form, yet in point of fact, and from the nature of the case, it becomes *affirmative* testimony. The imputation that he was an accomplice and a participator in the plunder was also unsupported. He went to the Convent with a good motive — to look after the safety of the women and children; and he took possession of a number of valuable articles, to rescue them from destruction. That this was his design, was shown by the proof that he sent a message to the priest, informing the latter that he had the property in his possession. His being a Catholic, and a regular member of Mr. Byrne's congregation, precluded the presumption that he was in the Convent for plunder; and if the jury believed him, in all the particulars of his testimony, and thought he was not mistaken, then the defendant was guilty.

With respect to Buck, His Honor agreed with the Attorney General, that the tendency of admitting the evidence of accomplices was beneficial to the community, by destroying the confidence in each other which criminals might otherwise feel; and the fact that Buck did not attempt to implicate Buzzell in every transaction he witnessed, as a corrupt witness might be expected to do, was also adverted to. His Honor also alluded to the circumstance that the prisoner made no attempt to prove an *alibi;* nor did it appear that he was at home that night.

Mr. Mann, counsel for Buzzell, suggested to His Honor, that in going over the evidence, the testimony of John R. Smith was not mentioned.

Judge Shaw observed that the suggestion was a very proper one, as the testimony of Smith was important. He was at the gate late, and saw a man whom he at first thought was Buzzell; and he became satisfied it was not the prisoner. It was also proper to make a general remark. The burden of the proof was on the government. It must not only prove the crime from evidence, but bring it home to the prisoner. The proof, however, was to be such as the nature of the case admitted. Strong presumption may be sufficient, if uncontradicted by other circumstances. But such circumstances may entirely explain it away, and change the presumption to the side of innocence.

The Judge reviewed the whole evidence, from its commencement to its close, occupying a large part of two days in his address; and told the jury that they were to set aside all prejudice; to be wholly uninfluenced by the existing state of the public mind; to care nothing about what other persons might think of them, and be the consequences what they might, fall where they might, to give such a verdict in the case as truth and their consciences dictated.

Having presented to the jury the considerations which, as he told them, he believed to embrace all the law and evidence most material to the case, the Chief Justice said to them, "In coming to your conclusion, gentlemen, with all the deliberation and impartiality which you will feel it incumbent on you to exercise on so important a cause, you will consider, — First: Has the crime been committed? Second: What species of crime was it? Third: Was it the result of combination, concert, or conspiracy? and, Fourth: Whether the defendant was aiding and assisting in that crime?" In conclusion, the Chief Justice said, —

"As far as I know, the court have now discharged their duty; it remains for you to discharge yours. It is one of great magnitude. The laws must be enforced, the security of life and property must be preserved; but this must be done by punishing the guilty, not the innocent. To insure this result, you should divest yourselves of every influence that can lead to a bias on one side, or the other, not founded on the law or evidence; setting aside all prejudice, all partiality, all considerations of the public approbation or disapprobation. Let the single inquiry of your consciences be, Is the prisoner proved guilty? This is your duty; and having done it faithfully and impartially, I am sure that whatever the consequences may be, you can have no cause to regret them."

The jury returned precisely at twelve o'clock on the 11th. Mr. Farley made a complaint to the court of the daily reports of the testimony, with comments thereon, which had appeared in the papers, and moved an order to prohibit further publication until the trials were closed. He did not make this motion at first, because he did not see the effect of such reports upon the cause. The court took time to consider the motion, and on the 12th refused to grant it. The Chief Justice said it would always be proper for the press to conform to the rules of the court relative to such publications; but so long as only facts were given, the court really had no power over publishers out of court. Judge Shaw suggested caution in conforming to the facts, and in avoiding comments of an injurious tendency.

THE ACQUITTAL. — THREATS AND DEMONSTRATIONS.

The Attorney General renewed his efforts to have the other trials continued to the next term. He spoke of the great excitement created by publications in the newspapers by witnesses, editors, &c., alluding particularly to statements by Messrs. Runey and Edward Cutter, which had appeared in the Charlestown Aurora; of threatening handbills, and the absence of witnesses. To mitigate the hardship that might accrue to the prisoners, he would not oppose their being admitted to bail. Edward G. Prescott, of their counsel, observed, that it was a great hardship to send respectable men and young boys through the streets, with a halter round their necks, to be drawn up at the beck of the Attorney General. Mr. Prescott replied that the Lady Superior began the publication of these exciting appeals, and the Attorney General ought to have restrained her. He insisted upon proceeding to try the other cases. The court decided that the grounds for continuance were not sufficient.

One of these inflammatory handbills, printed in large type, was exhibited in court, and commenced in the following style:

"LIBERTY OR DEATH!
"SUPPRESSED EVIDENCE.
"Sons of Freedom! Can you live in a free country, and bear the Yoke of Priesthood, veiled in the habit of a profligate Court?" &c.

Mr. Austin was styled a "Catholic Myrmidon," Judge Fay a "Prejudiced Probate Judge," and the handbill concluded by a threat that the mob would take the law into their own hands if the prisoners were not acquitted. The court treated the document with contempt and indifference. Judge Fay, besides giving his evidence in the case, had been drawn into some newspaper controversy on the subject.

At ten o'clock, on the 12th, the jury came in with a verdict of acquittal of Buzzell, having been out twenty-two hours. A loud clapping of hands, and other manifestations of approval, followed from the assembled citizens, and two of them, named Flanders and Ford, were arrested by the Sheriff, when the demonstration ceased. They made oaths before the court of their ignorance of any impropriety in their expressing their approval of the verdict, and were discharged. Buzzell was also discharged, though there was another indictment against him. He left the court room, accompanied by a crowd. The intelligence was brought over to Boston by some excitable anti-Catholic, who went galloping through the streets, waving his hands, and shouting "Acquitted! Acquitted!"

The intelligence of the result was received with some surprise in the city, since the evidence, which was published daily, was considered to be strongly against the prisoner. It was explained afterwards, that upon the first balloting of the jury they stood five for acquittal to seven for conviction. In the morning, before they left their room, they stood ten for acquittal and two for conviction; but on the way from their room to the court-house the two suddenly changed their minds, and agreed to acquit the prisoner. The trial of Buzzell was considered a test case, for he had been selected as a known and prominent ringleader in the attack and burning, and if the crime could not be legally brought home to him, his less active associates were not likely to be in danger.

CHAPTER III.

CONTINUATION OF THE TRIALS. — MASON, MARCY, AND BLAISDELL.

AT the conclusion of the Buzzell trial, after the excitement had been allayed, and order had been restored, Attorney General Austin again moved the court for a continuance of the trials. The state of excitement existing in relation to them — a specimen of which they had just witnessed — rendered it impossible, he said, that the ends of justice could be at this time accomplished. The court, however, decided that they saw no reason to alter the opinion they had previously expressed upon this point, and the proceedings went on.

The officers were directed to bring in William Mason, Marvin Marcy, Jr., and Sargeant Blaisdell, for whom Messrs. Prescott and Derby were counsel. The counsel claimed that the prisoners, though tried together, should each have the usual privilege of challenging twenty jurors, which was assented to by the court, though very few challenges were made; and the jury were impanelled, with John B. Goodwin, of

Lowell, as foreman. The others were Luther Barrett, Watertown; George Bancroft, Reading; Harvey Reeves and William Sherman, East Sudbury; Levi Farwell, Cambridge; Gilbert Haven, Malden; Simon Hosmer, Jr., Acton; Joseph Tapley and William N. Owen, Lowell; Jabez D. Parker, Reading; Timothy Smith, Westford.

District Attorney Huntington opened the case, and called Bishop Fenwick, who merely testified concerning the ownership of the Convent, and explained the situation of the buildings and apartments upon a plan before the court.

Godfrey de Gilse, brother-in-law to Miss Harrison, and a watchmaker, of Bowdoin Square, Boston, was on the stand a long time, — the first and second days of the trial, — and much interest was taken in his testimony. The principal object of the government in introducing him was to convict Mason, whom De Gilse recognized as one of the incendiaries. He and some friends went over from Boston twice that night, the first time about half past eight o'clock. Then, there were some two hundred persons collected at the Convent gate, and he and his party were asked if they came to help them; but no reply was given; and then they were told, that if they would wait a few minutes a body of brick-makers would be raised to pull the Convent down. His party followed the mob, at a little distance behind, up to the Convent, when the latter paraded themselves in front, occupying the whole line of the paling. A lady (not the Superior) appeared at the window, and talked about five minutes with the mob, who then seemed about to retire. His party spoke to the inmates, and said, "We came to protect them." The Lady Superior, who had then come to the window, said they needed no aid; that God was their protector; and she told the mob they had better go away. They retorted in blackguard language, and told her they wanted to see the "concealed lady;" to which she replied that they might see her if they would call the next morning; but not then. After further conversation, the mob threatened the Superior that if the lady was not produced they would tear down the house. The mob retired, and his party followed.

Mr. Runey, of the Selectmen, was very near to them. The mob increased, and called De Gilse and his friends spies and nullifiers, and the latter returned home. He went back to the Convent about twelve o'clock, accompanied by Miss Harrison's own brother. When he first went off he understood from the mob that nothing would be done till Thursday night, and so he made no efforts to protect the Convent. Buildings were on fire when he arrived the second time, and all was confusion. He and Mr. Harrison went to Mr. Cutter's house, but were not allowed to see the nuns. The mob had informed them of Miss Harrison's safety.

Aaron L. Dennison, a fireman, who had been referred to by the last witness as having endeavored to prevent Mason from setting fire to the ice-house, was examined, but did not identify the prisoner. Daniel J. Coburn, who arrested Mason, testified to finding a piece of plate in his possession, taken from the Convent. Mason's mother had burned some pictures which he had brought home from the fire. Quite a number of witnesses were examined to prove young Marcy's connection with the mob and burning.

Joseph L. Drew, who is well known as an ex-Alderman of the city of Boston, and also for many years connected with the school committee and assessors' department, was a member of Engine Company No. 13, then located near the Old Jail in Leverett Street. This was the Boston company nearest to the fire; and its members were accused, not only of sympathizing with the rioters, but of actually assisting in the destruction; but nothing of the kind was proved at the trial.

Mr. Drew was called by the prosecution to describe the proceedings, and to identify the prisoners. He went over with the engine, which was received with cheers by the crowd; but it was common at this time to cheer the Boston engine company which arrived first at an out-of-town fire. The mob — brick-makers and others — at once seized the ropes, and dragged the engine up to the front of the house. There was then a bonfire outside, and Captain Quinn ordered his men to take the engine back to the Convent gate, as he was not desirous to be implicated in the affair. There they remained till three o'clock the next morning. Wilbur, who was indicted, but had not been taken, was a volunteer, who sometimes went with the engine. Mr. Drew was sent several times to the Convent to see if any of the members were there, and if so, to order them back to the engine. He saw Wilbur in the top of the building, having a torch, and looking out of a small window.

Joseph Hunnewell, one of the Selectmen, was introduced, as the Attorney General said, to show the conduct of the engine-men at the fire. He came out of his house in Charlestown at the first alarm, and a messenger having come from the Convent with the information that "it was only a bonfire," he endeavored, without avail, to stop the Boston engine-men from proceeding any farther. As they passed him, some one remarked, "This is not all going to end in a bonfire."

Quite a number of witnesses were called for the purpose of identifying the prisoners at the bar as members of the mob; but their testimony was not conclusive, except that young Marcy had admitted to one of them that he knocked a book off at "auction," and threw it into the fire. Many witnesses "believed" that they saw Mason and Marcy among the rioters, but were not positive.

On the morning of the 15th, the Lady Superior was placed upon the stand again; but her direct testimony was only a repetition of what she had said before. She was laboring under indisposition, her voice was faint and low, and Mr. Austin was obliged to sit beside her, and repeat her answers to the court. Her cross-examination, however, related to the circumstance mentioned by De Gilse — that early in the evening a lady addressed the mob from the window, and her observations almost induced them to disperse; that he and others offered the lady their protection, upon which the Superior appeared at another window, and told them she did not require to be protected. The Superior explained that she thought they were in liquor, and were not to be depended upon; and she told them she would depend on the protection of God.

She explained that the male servants ate, drank, and slept at the farm-house; that the lay Sisters were those who, having taken the black veil, attended to the domestic concerns; the funds of the institution were understood to be for purposes of instruction, but they might be diverted from that object; if she should die or vacate her office, another Superior would be chosen by the Sisterhood, who must be confirmed by the Bishop; the finances of the institution were mostly exhausted by the erection of the building at Mount Benedict. Her worldly name was Grace O'Boyle; her religious one, Sister Bernard.

Miss Mary Ann Barber, whose religious name was Mary Benedict Joseph, and Mary Rebecca Theresa De Costa, otherwise called Mary Clare, identified a piece of silver plate, said to have been taken by Mason from the altar, with the pedestal of a cross. Their testimony related principally to matters which had been gone over before. Miss De Costa, who had not been before the court previously, described the attack upon the Convent, as she saw it. She saw the rioters as they came up to the institution, and went through the grounds and buildings. She went to the garden to join her friends and protectors, but suddenly remarked that one of the *Religieuses* had fainted away, and returned to see if the latter was safe. The Superior was not at the summer-house when the witness arrived there, and did not return for twenty minutes.

James Logan, who was a witness against Buzzell, identified Mason and Marcy as being at the fire. Saw Mason assist in bringing clothes and other articles, and throw them on a fire in one of the rooms; and saw Marcy sell the Bishop's books at mock auction.

A few unimportant witnesses were examined, and the government testimony was closed.

The Defence.

On the 16th, Mr. E. Hersey Derby opened the case for the defence, speaking four hours, after which he introduced testimony exculpatory of Mason; among his witnesses were four members of Charlestown Engine Company No. 4, to which Mason belonged. They flatly contradicted Logan as to Mason's manner of dress the night of the fire, and as was remarked at the time, "there must be gross perjury somewhere." The 17th and the greater part of the 18th were consumed in the same manner. The burning of the Convent ice-house, which was set on fire several times, and which was attempted to be fixed on Mason, was described by several of the witnesses. The rioters would bring fire, rags, or hay from the Convent, applying it to the eaves, and ram it in among the shingles. Firemen extinguished this, as often as it was started; and some of the rioters were thrown back by an engine-man, and they threw fire at him in return. The sacking of the Convent was described by some witnesses, who saw an image of the Saviour thrown from a window, which brought out the exclamation, "Here's a Jesus!" and saw Mason pick up the piece of plate. Other witnesses testified to the flight of Marcy, and his arrest at New Bedford, where he went to get on board a whaler. The character of Logan was again most essentially torn to pieces by quite a number of witnesses. One of them swore that he saw Logan pull down the balusters from the stairs, and throw them on a fire in one of the rooms. Mr. Austin declined to call witnesses again in favor of Logan, and said he should not press his evidence upon the jury.

This closed the evidence for the defence.

Edward G. Prescott then addressed the jury at length in defence of the prisoners. He asked them to take into consideration the state of feeling existing on all sides in relation to the institution, and to remember that the rioters were ignorant men, acting under the instigation of individuals better educated, and moving in a higher sphere than themselves. Also, to look at the conduct of the mob; their anxiety to save from injury the feeble inmates of the institution. The case was not marked, he said, with those features of malignity and turpitude described by the Attorney General.

Mr. Prescott concluded his defence at ten o'clock on the 18th, making a strong appeal to the jury in behalf of the innocence of his clients. He was followed by Attorney General Austin, in what was stated at the time to be one of the closest, most forcible, and most impressive arguments ever addressed to a jury; delivered, too, with a quiet eloquence and grace that rendered it more startling and remarkable. He commented with great severity upon the conduct of the gentlemen of the defence, in appealing to the feelings of the jury as regarded the consequences that might result from their verdict to the friends and relatives of the prisoners and to the prisoners themselves. If the whole world depended upon their "Yes" or "No," they were still bound to decide from the facts of the case. He was listened to with great attention in his general remarks, when he proceeded to the consideration of the evidence against the prisoners, and closed a little before four o'clock, P. M.

On the morning of the 20th, Judge Putnam delivered the charge to the jury, which was an able and impartial one, and they retired about eleven o'clock. They returned in the afternoon, with a verdict of *acquittal* in the cases of Blaisdell and Mason, but the foreman stated that they were unable to agree with regard to Marcy. Instructions upon certain points of law were given to them in relation to the case of Marcy by Judge Shaw, and they again retired. At a little before seven they came in again, stated they were still unable to agree, and were accordingly discharged. Thus ended three weeks of open trials, in addition to the elaborate investigations of the grand jury, and the government had accomplished nothing in the way of conviction. It was no wonder that the Attorney General was chagrined and discouraged at this great consumption of labor to no purpose.

POND, PARKER, KELLEY, AND MARCY.

On the morning of the 21st the trials recommenced, with Prescott P. Pond, Isaac Parker, Alvah Kelley, and Marvin Marcy, Jr., the last being included to give him a new trial before the next term of the court. It was stated at that time, with regard to Pond, the brother-in-law of Miss Rebecca Theresa Reed, that the grand jury, which met at Concord, and made the presentment, failed to find a bill against him, which so affronted Attorney General Austin, that he declared he would discharge them, and call for the impanelling of a new jury if Pond were not indicted. The consequence was, a bill was found against him by a majority of one. He was known to be a bitter enemy of the institution and its managers.

The Attorney General, who had experience of the futility of attempting to obtain convictions against the prisoners upon a capital charge, now proposed a *nolle prosequi* on all the counts of the indictment excepting one; that charging the prisoners with the commission of *arson;* and this one he proposed to modify in such a way that it should not be considered a capital charge. He was willing, he said, to concede that there were no persons lawfully in the Convent at the time it was set on fire. This motion of the Attorney General, if acceded to by the court, would have had the effect of depriving the prisoners of the peremptory power of challenge, to which all are entitled under a capital charge; and would also have exonerated the government from the obligation of assigning counsel for the prisoners; leaving the latter, of course, at liberty to employ such counsel as they thought proper.

The court decided against Mr. Austin's motion to modify the charge of arson, saying it was entirely a matter of evidence. It was for the jury to decide from the testimony adduced before them whether there was or was not any person in the building at the time it was set on fire. A jury was impanelled, with Joseph Bancroft as foreman.

In opening the case for the government, the Attorney General stated, that he was happy to tell the jury that the crime was not capital, as he admitted that at the time of the firing of the Convent there was not, according to the construction of the law by the court during the present trials, any person *lawfully* within that building. For the information of the jury, Mr. Austin read extracts, first from the statute of 1804, making the offence capital, and secondly from the mitigating statute of 1831. The Attorney General necessarily went over much ground which he had occupied in other trials, and he reiterated his admisson that the alleged offence came within the provisions of the mitigating statute, saying that he did not expect to be able to prove that either of the prisoners actually applied the brand of fire to the Convent. He asserted, however, that Kelley was present at the kindling of the signal bonfire, and gave his consent to have it built upon his land; that Pond knew of the intention to attack the Convent, and he came to the scene, and did enough there to implicate him; that Marcy, with the thoughtlessness of a boy, or the wickedness of a fiend, was present in every part of the building; and when it was too warm for him to remain there any longer, that he went to the Bishop's library, and assisted in the mock auction which preceded the destruction of the books. As to Parker, Mr. Austin stated that he acted a still more inferior part, but sufficiently important to bring him within the censure of the law.

The first government witness was David Buck, whose testimony only reached Alvah Kelley, the brick manufacturer for whom Buzzell worked. He declared that Kelley was present at the second meeting held to discuss the subject of tearing down the Convent; and he proposed to put off the attack for three weeks, to afford the directors of the Convent time to liberate the nun supposed to be held in durance within the institution against her will. He was to give notice if anything was to be done before the time. Also, Kelley suggested the building of the bonfire on his own land on the night of the riot; he directed the rioters to procure fire from his own house, and they forbore to use his fence for the bonfire because he had given them leave to build it on his land. Buck said, "I saw the fire brought from Kelley's house." He was very severely cross-examined, and some of his statements caused amusement in the court-house as they were drawn from him by Mr. Farley. When he was arrested, his employer, Captain Charles Adams, told him he was a "gone" one — that is, equal to a *dead* one. He said in return, "I can turn State's evidence, can't I?" Again: "When I was twelve years old the Selectmen of Claremont *gave* me to the Shakers at Enfield, and they *owned* me about a year, when my mother took me away because she didn't like." Also, he changed his name at Concord to William Henry Marsh, because he thought it was a "prettier sounding" one than Henry Buck. His cross-examination took a very wide range, and lasted into the next day, his credibility being severely attacked.

Among the witnesses were Bishop Fenwick, Godfrey De Gilse, and Elbridge Gerry, but their testimony was mostly a repetition of that given previously. The Sisters, Mary Ann Barber, who said she was a native of Connecticut, and Mary De Costa, a native of Boston, were also on the stand.

Edward Cutter met Kelley on the Saturday night prior to the burning, and told the latter that he had just seen the Lady Superior and Mary John — the lady that ran away; the "Mysterious Lady," as she was sometimes called. That Mary John was happy, and contented to stay there. Kelley said, "I and my family are acquainted there, and we will go up to-morrow and inquire." To some remark of Cutter's, that Kelley should take a proper way, he replied, "You may stand up for the —— Irish in their deviltry as much as you have a mind to, but I can't get along with it, and there will be —— to pay."

Michael Morrissey had had many conversations with Kelley about the Nunnery, against which the latter was very much prejudiced. He said it was a bad institution, and ought not to be allowed in a free country; that Bonaparte destroyed such institutions; that Catholics in general were a set of rascals and scoundrels; that the institution ought to come down; that nuns were kept there for a bad purpose; that the Bishop and priests pretended to live without wives, but the nuns were kept to supply their places. His language was "more vulgar" than this. He alluded to the nunneries of Europe, and said this one was similar to them. About a week before the riot, Kelley said, "If the lady that eloped does not get her liberty in a few days the Convent shall come down; but the time has not expired in which they promised to deliver her up." Her friends, even her brothers, Kelley said, had called at the Convent to see her, but they could get no satisfaction or admittance. Buzzell was present at some of these conversations. Kelley admitted that the Superior and himself were good friends, and he had always found her a good neighbor. Kelley and Buzzell both said they would give fifty dollars to any man who would pull the Convent down. Of this evidence, it may be said, that Kelley was probably irritated when he used the language attributed to him; but his opinions were the same as those of many ignorant or prejudiced persons at that time.

William T. H. Duncan, of Boston, who went over to the Convent on the night of the fire, asked some engine-men whom he met what the matter was, and was told, "There is a fire at the Convent; go ahead and pull it down." He had heard in Boston, at six o'clock that evening, that the Convent was to be destroyed; and some of the men whom he saw at the work of destruction were disguised.

The testimony of Captain James Quinn, of Boston Engine Company No. 13, about which so much had been said, excited considerable interest, and, as it was said at the time, "he gave it with great clearness, in a voice like a trumpet call." It might also be said that some of his expressions were couched in "language not suited to ears polite," letting alone the dignity of the Supreme Court of Massachusetts. Captain Quinn disclaimed all previous knowledge on the part of himself and his company of any intention to fire or attack the Convent. His testimony in relation to the scenes upon the first arrival of the engine at the Convent was corroborative of that of Mr. J. L. Drew; that the mob laid hold of the ropes of the engine, and drew it up to the Convent front, when the company was cheered. Stones began to be thrown by the mob in the shrubbery and the people who had thrown themselves upon the engine ropes; and Captain Quinn asked the multitude, "What in —— does all this mean?" A voice came from the shrubbery, "This is the Nunnery." The witness replied, "The devil it is!" He then gave the order to his company to man the ropes, and take the engine down to the road, which order was obeyed. Then he told the men that he would hold them responsible for any outrage which they might commit on the building or its furniture if they went up to the scene of riot.

At that time they had with them Captain Charles S. Clark, an engineer of the Boston Fire Department, and Captain Quinn's superior officer. The Charlestown engines had gone home, and the mob had full possession of the house.

On the 24th, Mr. Austin introduced five witnesses to identify certain anonymous handbills, posted up in different places, and others received by the Charlestown Selectmen, threatening the destruction of the Convent and the lives of the witnesses who might give evidence against the rioters. Copies of some of them are appended. One was headed in large type: —

"TO THE SELECTMEN OF CHARLESTOWN.

"Gentlemen: It is currently reported that a misterious affair has lately occured at the *Nunery* in Charlestown; now it is your duty, gentlemen, to have this affair investigated immediately, if not, the Truckmen of Boston will demolish the Nunery on Thursday night.

"*Boston, Aug.* 9, 1834."

Another was presented, which was nearly identical in character with the above. A third is given as a curiosity: —

"Go Ahead! To Arms!! To Arms!! Ye brave and free the Avenging Sword unshield!! Leave not one stone upon another of that curst Nunnery that prostitues female virtue and liberty under the garb of holy Religion. When Bonaparte opened the Nunnerys in Europe he found cords of Infant sculls!!!!!!"

The following was printed and posted up on old Charlestown Bridge: —

"All persons giving any information in any shape, or testifying in Court against any one concerned in the late affair at Charlestown, may expect *assassination* according to the oath which bound the party to each other."

It may be added here, that at the time when this evidence was offered in the court in East Cambridge, the Selectmen of Roxbury, in which town the Ursuline Community had taken refuge, being informed that the house occupied by the Lady Superior was threatened with destruction, like that of Charlestown, established a nightly watch, and offered a reward of five hundred dollars for the arrest of any disturber of the peace.

Quite a number of witnesses were called, who identified Parker pretty closely as being in the mob, and wearing a disguise. One of Pond's workmen and others testified to the great interest which he took in the affair, both before and during the destruction. Mr. David Kimball, who was then an engineer of the Boston Fire Department, described the disguises of the rioters, and the dresses which the mob assumed after their work was over, when a large number formed in procession to march from the north end of the building. Many of them were in grotesque female dress, wearing stolen feminine habiliments.

The testimony against young Marcy was very strong. It was proved that he was a leader in the mischief; that he had conversed about his own doings therein, saying to one man, "We went from garret to cellar, to see that no one was in the building before we set it on fire;" and that he attempted to ship on board a whaler at New Bedford, under a disguised name. Much of the evidence was merely recapitulatory of that which had been given before; and it was evident at this time that the interest of the community in the trials began to abate.

On the 26th the government closed its evidence in the case, and Mr. Prescott opened in defence of the prisoners in a speech of two hours; after which the testimony for the defence — explanatory, contradictory, and exculpatory — was introduced. There was a large amount of it, — good, bad, and indifferent, — but it was not of such a character as to require repeatal. The whole of Kelley's household, — mother, wife, sister, servants, and boarders, — as well as his neighbors, proved a pretty efficient *alibi* for him. His family swore he was in bed before the bonfire was lighted; which was in direct contradiction of former evidence before the jury.

Mr. Farley commenced the closing argument for the prisoners about ten A. M. on the 27th, and it lasted till half past four P. M., being pronounced at the time " perhaps the most matter-of-fact one ever addressed to a jury." He denied in the outset the existence of any deep-laid conspiracy, or that the Convent would ever have been demolished if the Superior had not imprudently denounced the collection around it as " vagabonds." He was very severe upon Buck, the State's evidence, whom he charged with direct perjury; his testimony was not to be read, or even talked about; his attempt to escape from jail, after he had testified before the magistrates and the grand jury, was a proof that he lied, and that he feared his falsehood would be discovered; he was known from his childhood as "a lying boy." Mr. Farley then proceeded to examine the evidence against Marcy, which he attempted to explain consistently with the latter's innocence, and to show that government witnesses were mistaken with respect to his connection with the affair. With regard to his *alias*, Mr. Farley declared that it was nothing uncommon for wild and thoughtless young men to change their names when taking to the sea.

In relation to young Parker, Mr. Farley suggested that the Attorney General should admit that a case was not made out against him, or that the court should declare the evidence to be insufficient. Mr. Austin said he should ask for a verdict against Parker on the evidence, but he would not argue upon the testimony if Mr. Farley would not. Mr. Farley did not accept this proposition, and argued that it was proved that Parker was not upon the scene till between two and three o'clock, and then only in obedience to his master's orders. His throwing a few stones at the windows of the dilapidated building was not proof of malice. Mr. Farley did not allude to the "only humane action proved to have been performed on that dreadful night, viz., Parker's saving a *hen* from being burned at the firing of the barn."

Mr. Farley was very ingenious in his explanations with respect to Pond, who had told one of the witnesses, "All I did was to say, 'Off badges and go ahead!'" He was extremely sarcastic with regard to the government witnesses, one of whom was a sheriff's officer, who had been placed as keeper in Pond's shop. Having gone minutely into the testimony relating to Marcy, Parker, and Pond, Mr. Farley took up the case of Alvah Kelley, and dissected and combated the evidence against him, his connection with the bonfire, &c., with great skill. Colonel Gerry's identifying Kelley as the individual who was present at the ring, and proposing a postponement till Thursday, from the "peculiar manner in which his head was placed upon his shoulders," was ridiculed by Mr. Farley in the most amusing manner; and he kept the court in a roar of laughter by his illustrations of the absurdity of the reason assigned for recognizing the accused. He was very hard upon the Stoneham Colonel, who had never explained how it was that he himself came to be at the rioting. The whole speech was admitted to be a masterpiece at the time of its delivery.

On the 29th Mr. Austin made his final argument against the prisoners, occupying nearly all the day. He described the alleged offence, and the law outraged by it, the crime being one that no man of reputation dared to palliate. He observed that a religion, which is that of more than half of Christendom, and which was for more than thirteen hundred years the sole depository of Christianity, could not be so horrible as to justify the burning of one of its institutions in the night. In proof of the existence of a conspiracy, which had been denied by the prisoners' counsel, the Attorney General referred to the extent to which the intended attack was known throughout Boston and the neighboring towns, and he read the threatening letters, &c., which have been noticed. He endeavored to sustain Buck's character and testimony, and was happy in alluding to one witness against the latter, who called himself a merchant, but on cross-examination admitted that he was a pedler, and Mr. Austin said, "was just the man to make mountains out of molehills." He commenced with the case of Kelley, and was quite severe upon his "family witnesses." He pressed the testimony of the government witnesses; argued that Kelley, whose house was nearest to the scene of disturbance, was in the conspiracy; and those who were wicked enough to form the conspiracy against the Convent were wicked enough to enter into a conspiracy to make evidence for their friends.

Mr. Austin was quite brief, though decisive, in commenting upon the testimony relating to Parker and Marcy, and expressed his regret that the latter did not escape on the whaling voyage, during which he would have suffered all the penalties, without the disgrace, of a sentence to the State Prison.

Having obtained a short adjournment, Mr. Austin proceeded

to argue and direct the evidence against Pond, whom he described as an enemy to the Convent, as was proved by three witnesses, and he was there with hostile intentions. The Attorney General paid a handsome compliment to Engine Company No 13, saying, "A worthier man than Captain Quinn, or a better company, does not exist in Boston; but an attempt was made to make tools of them, and this fact is the key to the whole transaction." He closed with Pond, by putting him to the jury as having a knowledge of the intended crime prior to its commission; as having a hostile feeling to the institution and its religion; as being upon the scene early, before the alarm of fire; as joining in the general scheme; using encouraging language, going with the crowd, urging them on, and never giving a satisfactory account of himself. He instructed the jury, in the most solemn terms, to divest themselves of every suggestion or influence from all outside sources.

At the conclusion of the Attorney General's argument, the prisoners having all declared that they had nothing to offer in addition to what their counsel had advanced in their defence, Judge Morton proceeded to charge the jury. He alluded to Kelley's hostility to the Catholic religion in general, and to the Convent in particular, as proved before them, and reviewed Buck's testimony against him, which was to be believed if he was generally corroborated. He concluded his charge on the 30th, reviewing the evidence relating to the other prisoners. The jury retired about eleven o'clock, and on the morning of the 31st came into court with a verdict of guilty against the lad Marcy; of acquittal for Parker; and they disagreed in relation to Pond and Kelley. Parker was discharged. Marcy, who was not convicted on the capital charge, after an ineffectual attempt of his counsel for a new trial, was remanded for sentence on the 25th of February, at which time Pond and Kelley were to have new trials.

The court decided to admit Pond and Kelley to bail in the sum of six thousand dollars each, and they were set at large. Nathaniel Budd, Jr., son of a baker in Boston, who had been indicted but not taken, appeared at the close of the session, and was bailed in five thousand dollars. Of all those arrested, no one was in prison save the boy Marcy; and of him Mr. Austin, in his chagrin at the failure of his efforts to convict the principals or leaders, had expressed a wish, in the open court, that he had escaped, to suffer the hardships and discomforts of a whaling voyage, when it was apparent that he was to be the only victim to the demands of justice. Marcy's counsel fought very hard for a new trial for him, on the ground that the jury had visited a barber's shop where there was a paper containing the trial, and had also been to the glass works, where they listened to conversation on the trial, but the court refused the motion.

In reference to the falling off of the interest of the people in the trials, after Buzzell's case was disposed of, a Boston daily paper, which had discontinued its reports, said,—

"The Convent trials, which were the first news asked for a few days ago, cannot now command attention for a paragraph of ten lines. Their majesty, the public, have settled the matter in their minds that the pirates are to be hung, and the Convent rioters to be acquitted, and so they wish no further information on the subject."

The "pirates" were Bernardo De Soto and six associates, who were tried in the U. S. Court at Boston, and convicted of piracy, and sentenced to be hanged, about the time of the Buzzell trial. De Soto was pardoned by President Jackson.

CHAPTER IV.

MARCY'S SENTENCE AND ITS REMITTAL. — THE END OF THE TRIALS. — REVIEW.

AT the reassembling of the court, February 25, 1835, the sentence of young Marcy was pronounced, which was three days solitary confinement in the State Prison, and imprisonment at hard labor for life. The court refused to admit David Buck, the State's evidence, to bail, and remanded him to prison, until the recurrence of the trials, which were again postponed to the regular term of the court, which was to be holden at Concord in April. It may be that the personal appearance as well as the indifferent character of Buck led to this discrimination against him, after the accused had been bailed by their friends, for he was as revolting and abject looking an individual as could well be conceived of.

On the 26th of February, two petitions were presented to the Governor and Council for the pardon of young Marcy. One was handed in by the Lieutenant Governor; the other came from the hands of Bishop Fenwick, and contained six thousand eight hundred and twenty one names, which had been attached to it since eleven o'clock the previous day. A letter from the Lady Superior in behalf of herself and the Sisters, also petitions from Worcester, Cambridge, Medford, and several other towns, for the same purpose, were also presented. They were accompanied by various affidavits relating to the matter, which came from Mr. Farley, the counsel for the prisoner.

Young Marcy remained in prison over seven months. The Legislature had elected Governor John Davis, United States Senator; and acting Governor Samuel T. Armstrong and the Council remitted the sentence, October 8, 1835. The remitment was accompanied by some strict conditions, and he was never fully restored to citizen rights. The following record of the order for his release is copied from books of the Governor and Council.

"Upon full consideration in the premises, we do hereby remit to the said Marvin Marcy the residue of the punishment which he was sentenced to endure, on condition that within one day of his liberation from the State Prison he becomes bound to some good citizen of this Commonwealth, until he shall have reached the full age of twenty-one years, to learn some useful trade; and within the period of said apprenticeship shall not come within the distance of fifteen miles of the city of Boston, — of which all our judges, justices, magistrates, and officers of every denomination, and especially the Warden of the State Prison, are to take notice."

The time for the new trial of the prisoners again awoke the public interest in the events, which had apparently slumbered for a while, and some of their indiscreet associates exhibited their bad taste and temper in a manner thus noticed by the Transcript of April 7: "The friends of good order will feel humiliated at the knowledge that the American Flag was floating yesterday over the ruins of the Ursuline Convent at Charlestown!"

During the court vacation, also, the public mind had been excited by the appearance of Miss Reed's book, "Six Months in a Convent;" which was said to have been prepared or revised by a committee, and which had a heavy sale. The Transcript of April 10, said, "The answer of the Lady Superior to Miss Reed will be published to-morrow. The 'Committee of Publication' will have to go to work again. Miss Reed's book is knocked into *pi*.'" On the 15th it was stated that the Superior's answer to Miss Reed's book had received a rapid and extended sale, as the first edition of five thousand copies was immediately sold, and a second edition of the same number was nearly disposed of.

The court assembled at Concord in April, but civil cases only were tried. It adjourned, and met again May 19, but the criminal trials were not taken up until Tuesday, June 1, with Chief Justice Shaw and Judges Wilde and Putnam. Judge Morton held a court at Nisi Prius. Prescott P. Pond and Alvah Kelley were arraigned, with Aaron Hadley, Jr., of Charlestown, who had surrendered since the last trials, and Nathaniel Budd, Jr., as the court decided to put them all on trial at the same time. The court assigned Messrs. George F. Farley, of Groton, and S. H. Mann, of Lowell, as counsel for the defendants; and in addition, Messrs. Bradford Sumner and Justin Field appeared as counsel for Budd, and E. G. Prescott for Pond and Kelley. It was stated in the reports of the day of two of the prisoners, Budd and Hadley, that they were not more than seventeen or eighteen years of age, "and would have been called the handsomest young gentlemen in the court-house."

Very little difficulty was experienced in impanelling a jury, after which the trial proceeded. The case was opened by Attorney General Austin, on the part of the government, and he stated that all the counts in the original indictment, except the the first, had been abandoned, and that the case was not to be regarded as a capital one. He did not proceed against the prisoners on the capital offence; but merely for burning a dwelling-house in the night time.

On the first day, Bishop Fenwick was called to prove the ownership and the burning of the property; and several other witnesses were called to prove that threats had been current in Charlestown for seveal days before the deed, and that sundry handbills of a threatening character had been posted up.

The testimony against Pond and Kelley was almost the same as that which had been brought out at the December trials. Henry Buck, the State witness, was again on the stand; but his testimony did not appear to reach Budd or Hadley. Some evidence in relation to the former, as read now, appears to have been of rather a frivolous character, being reported thus: Maria Hall stated that Budd discussed the destruction of the Convent, "sometimes using the first and sometimes the third person plural," and that he once said, "We are going to burn all the Catholic churches." Mary Jones heard Budd say that he went to the fire, and he also told what they did there. Mary J. Pushard heard him say a few words of the burning, but did not say that he had a hand in it, or that he was present. Warren Towner heard Budd say he was "over there," but didn't hear him say he was in the house.

In reference to Hadley, Walter Balfour, Jr., testified that he saw him in three or four rooms of the Convent with a party having a lamp. Mr. Balfour went round with them, and thought they were trying to ascertain whether any one was left in the house. Hadley was doing nothing. This witness, together with John Wade, S. C. Hunt, and Edward Handy, spoke in high terms of Hadley's character. The new testimony in general was of very little account or interest, and was mostly technical.

The trials were conducted with more despatch than was allowed to those which preceded them. The argument in the case was closed on the part of the defendants, on Thursday P. M. of the 4th; the case was argued on the part of the government by Attorney General Austin, on the forenoon of Friday, the 5th, and the charge of the court was concluded at three o'clock in the afternoon. In about three hours the jury returned a verdict of acquittal of all the defendants.

Thus ended the famous Convent trials, which in their commencement, and during the early stages, excited a greater interest than has been accorded to any judicial investigations in Massachusetts for half a century at least. The interest in them, however, faded out before they concluded, and but little note was taken of the Concord trials except by those immediately interested. The end was by no means that which was expected at the beginning.

Conclusion.

About thirty-five years have passed away since the occurrence of the scenes and events which have been chronicled in these pages, and with them have passed also from life the greater portion of those who participated therein, directly or indirectly. The judges who sat at the December trials, Chief Justice Shaw and Judge Putnam, with Judge Morton, who was afterwards Governor of the State, all died some years ago; and the same is to be recorded of the venerable Judge Wilde, who sat at the closing trial. The counsel for the prisoners, Mr. Farley, the able lawyer, Mr. Mann, the eloquent advocate, Mr. Prescott, who afterwards took orders in the Episcopal Church, and who was brother to Prescott, the historian, and Mr. E. Hersey Derby, who may be remembered as the efficient agent of the banks in ferreting out counterfeiters, and who died in his vocation, having caught a malignant fever in Montreal — all are gone. The Attorney General, Mr. Austin, still survives, though he has long since retired from business, and his able assistant, Mr. Huntington, yet wears the harness of his profession in Essex County. The Convent Community, which was temporarily removed to the General Dearborn estate in Roxbury, was removed to Quebec, and it may be mentioned as a coincidence, that the Catholic Church has within a year or two purchased the same property, which is now used as a charitable asylum. The respected Bishop Fenwick and the Lady Superior are both deceased. Nothing appears to be known of Miss Harrison, whose eccentric conduct or whose infirmity was the main cause of the crime and disaster which followed. Her brother, William Harrison, was set down in the Boston Directory of 1834 as an engraver, but his name disappeared from the Directory after that year; and that of his brother-in-law, De Gilse, was never in it.

Of those who were arrested and placed upon trial, Buzzell died in New Hampshire some years afterwards, and it was stated in the newspapers of the time that he confessed his participation in the events of the Convent burning before his death. The confession was entirely supererogatory, for no one who was present at, or read the reports of the trial, would have any doubts in regard to his guilt, though that was not proved to the minds of the jury, or of a majority of the members thereof. Prescott P. Pond, the brother-in-law of Miss Reed, the authoress of "Six Months in a Convent," who was regarded as a prime originator and engineer in conceiving and carrying out the work of destruction, is understood to have been dead many years. He was a shoemaker in Federal Street, and his name disappeared from the Boston Directory in 1837. It was reported that he had removed to Providence. Of Mason, Parker, Budd, Blaisdell, Thurston, &c., we have no account. Marcy is now a useful citizen of New Hampshire. Mr. Hadley is still a resident of Charlestown. Mr. Edward Cutter and Mr. Adams, neighbors of the Convent Community, have been dead several years, but Mr. Fitch Cutter is yet living, and hale and hearty at the age of seventy-nine.

Of the Lady Superior, to whose stern and unyielding course during the excitement and difficulties which preceded the riot, the disaster has been often attributed, there have been strange and contradictory rumors, both before and since the time of the trials. She was a woman of masculine appearance and character, high-tempered, resolute, defiant, with stubborn, imperious will. There were disputes concerning her origin. She gave her "worldly" name at the trials as Grace O'Boyle, which would indicate Irish parentage; but Mr. Fitch Cutter, her neighbor, who knew her very well, and was frequently employed upon business affairs by her, always regarded her as an American woman. Notwithstanding all her faults of temper, she was respected by those who were acquainted with her, and even Alvah Kelley, who was among the most zealous enemies of her religion, and of the institution over which she presided, acknowledged that she was a "good neighbor." It was currently reported, and believed, that she was the daughter of Stephen Burroughs, the once noted rogue, so celebrated as a thief and counterfeiter. Burroughs was the son of a New Hampshire clergyman, was educated at Dartmouth College, and the book of his adventures, purporting to be written by himself, was very popular reading fifty years ago. In his older years he closed his career of counterfeiting, in which he was very expert, entered the communion of the Catholic Church, and passed his old age in receiving and educating, at his house in Three Rivers, Canada, the sons of wealthy gentlemen of the Province. He died in January, 1840, in the seventy-sixth year of his age. This may have been the foundation of the reports which made him father to the Ursuline Convent Superior. A venerable Sister of the Order, now living, has the impression that her name was Burrill; that she was born in Burlington, Vermont, and died in Canada. The similarity of the names of O'Boyle and Burrill may have been a reason for this confusion in regard to her. She was thrown out of her vocation by the burning of the Convent, and the Community have no after record in regard to her.

Mr. Walter Balfour, Jr., who was so much commended by Mr. Austin for the spirit which he displayed on the exciting occasion, is a citizen of Saratoga, N. Y.

It appeared to be evident to all who took an interest in the proceedings, that the Selectmen of Charlestown, at the time, were singularly inefficient; and that, knowing the threats and warnings which had been thrown out, they should have provided some defence against the dangers which had been foreshadowed. There were two Light Infantry Companies in the town at the time, and one of them, the "Warren Phalanx," had a very high military character. But the Selectmen were probably new to their duties. If memory be correct, they were chosen as "Workingmen," or bore some similar party designation; and besides, not being perfectly aware of their responsibilities, it is probable that they had no apprehension of the riot and destruction which was to follow their inaction or lack of precaution. It will be remembered that Judge Fay, of Cambridge, and the late Levi Thaxter, of Watertown, who had daughters at the Convent school, both rode over to the institution early in the evening of the occurrences of disorder, saw the incipient mob, and might have understood that there was to be trouble of some sort, and yet they rode home in company, without taking their children with them! There was a strange fatuity in all the proceedings.

The Convent walls, blackened by the conflagration, are still standing, and the once beautiful grounds are wild and desolate. The impression is, that these relics of mob misrule and recklessness are to remain thus for all time as a reproach to the State of Massachusetts, which has refused to pay for the property so wantonly destroyed, though her Legislature has enacted a law providing for such restitution in the future. At the first meeting of the citizens of Boston, on the day after the rioting, to express opinions upon this grave and startling outrage, Mr. George Bond, a gentleman who never rose in Faneuil Hall to utter his sentiments upon any subject without being listened to with attention and respect, suggested to those present the absolute propriety of providing means for remunerating all who had suffered losses through the mad proceedings of the night before. This manifestly just course of action was also advocated by various writers in the newspapers of the day, and the subject was at different times brought before the Legislature, but the majority was always found to be inexorably adverse to compensation. It may be that those who voted against the claim were influenced as much by sectarian as by pecuniary motives, and that justice was made secondary to expediency and a desire to retain popularity. At any rate, the Legislature has steadily refused to pay the bill incurred by the Convent rioters on the night of the 11th of August, though many look forward to the day when Massachusetts will wipe out this stain upon her escutcheon.

APPENDIX.

To the foregoing pages, may be added some opinions and remembrances, gathered in recent conversation with persons who were intimately connected with the events of the memorable night of the 11th of August, 1834.

FROM A PUPIL OF THE CONVENT SCHOOL.

Mrs. Mary Frances Canaday (*née* Peduzzi) was a pupil of the institution at the time covered by the circumstances which have been related, but she was on a visit to her home in Portsmouth, N. H., on the day of the destruction of the Convent. She is now a resident of Somerville, as she has been for some years. She was a sufferer pecuniarily, but not to the extent of many other pupils. She describes the instruction of the institution as being of the highest order; the teachers being extraordinary proficients in music, the languages, and in all the rare feminine accomplishments. The Lady Superior was an extraordinary French scholar and reader. Nothing of religious sectarianism was thought of at the school, and there were only about a dozen Catholics in the sixty or seventy scholars which formed the whole number. She conversed with several of her fellow-pupils, who described the first alarm of the night of terror as coming with the suddenness of a thunderbolt. No such event had been thought of, for under the discipline of the institution the scholars knew little or nothing of what passed in the house beyond their own pursuits and duties. Their description of the terrifying scenes of the night coincided with the accounts which were published in the papers of the time.

In relation to the temper and bearing of the Lady Superior,

Mrs. Canaday states that the pupils saw very little of her, their intercourse being nearly altogether with the different teachers. She was a dignified, well-bred lady, and was uniformly kind whenever she came in association with the scholars. All Mrs. Canaday's memories in reference to the Superior are favorable.

FROM FITCH CUTTER.

Mr. Fitch Cutter, who yet resides at his mansion opposite the deserted Convent grounds, has still a lively recollection of all the events of the night, as well as of those which preceded the terrible denouement. Notwithstanding all the threatenings and the excitement which preceded the storm, he had no idea that such a riot could be raised, or gathered, or that the destruction which ensued was to be wrought out. He is still firm in the opinion that had the Lady Superior been less defiant and intractable, and had come forward with Miss Mary John and the children, and appealed to the feelings, the good sense and magnanimity of the assembled miscellaneous crowd, the result would have been entirely different, and the painful and harrowing events of the night would never have been known. Mr. Cutter states that all his experience of the night is contained in an article written by one of the editors of the Bulletin, who had a recent interview with him, and the following is taken from his account of the flight of the inmates : —

"At eight o'clock, on the evening of August 11, 1834, the pupils of the Ursuline Convent, in obedience to the strict discipline which governed that institution, sought their dormitories. There were fifty-three pupils in all, and each detachment of them was constantly attended by a lay nun. With military promptness and regularity their simple preparations for the night were made; in a few minutes the little white beds received their respective tenants, and silence reigned in the spacious apartments. Most of the young creatures soon lapsed into the deep and sweet slumber of childhood. Upon some eyes in the dormitories, however, the drowsy god refused to brood, and some brains were busy in the silence with perplexing problems. Why, asked some of the older pupils, did these men [the Selectmen of Charlestown] come here to-day? And why, after seeing them, was the Lady Superior so fierce and harsh? What evil can be threatening us? But these questions found no answers, and, weary with wondering, the active brains relaxed and tired eyes closed, and presently the fifty-three pupils were all together in the Land of Nod.

"Suddenly there was a frightened awakening. Yells and cries were heard from the street, and the sound of many trampling feet. The riot had begun. Hastening from bed to bed the lay nuns roused the dazed sleepers, and bade them dress instantly. They obeyed, and being left for a moment to themselves, — their attendants, in the panic of the time, rushing hither and thither, seeking orders from the Superior, snatching up precious relics or valuable articles of silver for preservation, forgot all discipline and yielded to the whirl of confusing events, — they repaired to the front of the Convent and gazed out upon the mob below. Some two hundred men were there, many in disguise, all crazed with excitement; yells filled the air, torches lit up the scene with lurid light; the mob surged hither and thither, as mobs always do in incertitude. The timid girls looking down from those upper windows saw a photograph of Pandemonium. No wonder they shrank back, and sought each other's arms. There was no refuge for them, no comfort within. The Lady Superior, stern, undismayed, and unyielding, went about, directing her nuns and reviling the mob, at intervals. Some of the older pupils, recovering their self-possession, began to gather their property together and to prepare for departure, but the nuns forbade them to go.

"About ten o'clock the mob disappeared from the front of the Convent, and it seemed as if the perils of the night had passed; every face lighted up with hope, and even the lineaments of the Superior took on the look of relief. The pupils were ordered to return to the dormitories, and were on the way thither, when lights began to gleam at the lower end of the lawn. The bedward procession was halted. A moment more, and the mob marched upon the grounds in front of the Convent, armed with torches, and uttering the terrible cries that, heard in the night from the lips of an angry populace, strike terror to the boldest hearts. The old grimness came over the face of the Lady Superior at the sight, but she was still intrepid. 'Go down,' she said to the huddled pupils, 'go down to the front door, and show yourselves to the mob; the sight of you may quiet them.' Obedient, the pupils started; but during their passage from the third to the second story the attack began — the windows were broken in. Instantly the Lady Superior ordered the pupils to escape by the rear entrance. They set off at the moment, and as they passed through the long corridor, the fated Mary John joined their ranks and passed out with them. Hurrying helter-skelter, and aimlessly, for they had not been permitted to visit this portion of the grounds, and were ignorant of its character, they ran down a steep declivity, and were checked by a high and tight board fence. Over this, with much difficulty, the older pupils scrambled, tumbling into a potato-patch, and sped away towards Mr. Edward Cutter's house. The younger girls, vainly trying to surmount the fence, sank back upon the ground disheartened, and wept as the sound of retreating feet grew fainter.

"Reaching Mr. Cutter's house, the older pupils were instantly admitted, and that gentleman and George Johnson at once went back to aid the little ones. The reunited flock were safely lodged in some upper rooms.

"In a little time the Lady Superior and some of the nuns passed the house. Mr. Cutter asked her to come in, but the Superior refused to do so. He repeated his invitation; but she scorned it, and declared that she would go to Mr. Adams's house. He offered to escort her thither, but she refused to allow him to do so. He persisted, however, and when they arrived at the house, she said, 'Mr. Adams, I want you to let me in, not on Mr. Cutter's account, but on my own; I will have nothing to do with him.' Having established herself at Adams's, herself occupying an upper room, with the nuns below stairs, and all the lights extinguished, the Superior sent peremptory orders to the scholars to join her there. The older ones refused to obey. At dawn carriages came from Boston, and conveyed the pupils to that city.

"During the riot, when the inmates of the Convent had fled, and the building was in flames, a nun ran up to Mr. Fitch Cutter's house and begged for admission. He opened the door, and she asked for a place at a window where she could look out upon the fearful scene. Here she remained all night. Once she begged Mr. Cutter to go to a barn attached to the Convent, and release a horse therein; she feared the barn would be burned. He thought her fears were groundless; but yielding to her urgent solicitation, he went out and released the horse. Later in the night the nun requested Mr.

Cutter to go with her to recover a piece of plate, which belonged to the altar service of the Convent, and which in her flight from the burning building, she had cast into some currant bushes. He accompanied her to the designated spot, but their search was vain."

Mr. Cutter has the following to say with respect to the " mysterious lady," who was the prime cause of all the disaster: —

" One day, two or three weeks before the riot, Mary John came to his house, and desired him to carry her to Mr. Cotting's, in West Cambridge. It was inconvenient for him to comply with her request, and Mr. Runey consented to carry her that evening. She took tea at the house of Mr. Edward Cutter. At the table she said she had left the Convent forever, and no power on earth could force her to return; she was unwilling to make trouble, and in speaking of the institution maintained a careful reticence; she made no specific charges of ill treatment or wrong of any kind, but vaguely implied that it was not a pleasant place to live in. Mr. Runey arrived, and with his wife, Mr. Edward Cutter's daughter, and Mary John in his carriage, drove to West Cambridge. On his return, Runey went directly to the Convent, and informed the Lady Superior where he had left the fugitive. This happened on Saturday. A fortnight or more passed, during which various rumors touching the missing lady were abroad. It was reported that Bishop Fenwick had proposed to Mary John that she should return to the Convent, and at the end of three weeks should, if she desired, depart without let or hinderance."

Of the visit of himself and brother to the Convent, in consequence of the rumors outside relating to Mary John, he says, that they saw her, and adds: —

"'There,' said the Lady Superior to them, 'look at her — touch her — see if you can find any marks of violence — question her as you please — ask her if she has been punished.' Mary John turned back the sleeves of her dress to exhibit her arms, but no bruises were visible. Then she spoke, — this weak, capricious woman, whose insanity or wickedness was the direct cause of so much wrong, — and said, she had decided to remain in the Convent; it was her preference to remain; she was kindly treated, and had no complaint to make; she desired that this should be publicly stated. Only three weeks ago she had declared that no power on earth could force her to return to the Convent."

From Captain Quinn.

Captain James Quinn, now of the Boston Police, and Foreman of Engine Company No. 13 at the time of the riot, is very clear in his recollection of all the events which passed under his observation on the memorable night of August 30, 1834. He is of opinion now as then, that had the Charlestown authorities at that time set themselves resolutely at work to prevent the assembling of the rioters, after the warnings which they had received, and when they saw the first manifestations of the mob-spirit early in the evening, the unhappy occurrences could not have taken place. A determined leader, having official authority, with a dozen well-disposed and resolute men to aid him, could, in the opinion of Captain Quinn, have driven off the miscellaneous collection, which at that time appeared to have but little purpose or method, and with the authority of the law on their side they could have effectively preserved the peace, and prevented the commission of the crime and folly which followed. He states that he saw one of the Board of Selectmen standing by the Convent fence when he arrived with his Company upon the scene of tumult, but this official did not seem to comprehend either the situation of affairs or his own duty in the exigency. When the last of the trials were holden at Concord, Captain Quinn was present as a government witness, and he testified to this effect before the jury in answer to some questions by Attorney General Austin. He was asked then, why he did not interfere for the safety of property and the preservation of the peace; and he replied that he had no authority whatever. He was a Boston fireman, and could not even direct a stream of water upon a fire beyond the city limits, without orders from the local authorities. The Boston papers contained no reports of the Concord trials, except small paragraphs relating to the extent of their proceedings, which is the reason this part of his evidence was never published before.

Notwithstanding the compliment which was paid by Mr. Austin to the members of Engine Company No. 13, and their Foreman, in one of his speeches before the jury, Captain Quinn has been somewhat strangely accused of being connected with the riot and outrages, and the company was for a long time subjected to sneers and depreciatory remarks from persons who were unacquainted with the circumstances. The Board of Engineers of the Boston Fire Department ordered an official examination of the whole subject, so far as Boston enginemen were concerned, and appointed a sub-committee "to examine into the truth of various reports and allegations against certain members and companies of the Fire Department while on duty at the late fire in Charlestown." This committee attended to the duty, and submitted a report on the 27th of

August, 1834. Near the close of it they say, with respect to the conduct of the Company of No. 13,—

" The company, from the beginning, have courted investigation, being willing to undergo any examination required in Boston, Charlestown, or Cambridge, and have been subjected to great perplexity, inconvenience, and loss of time. No one who will candidly examine all the evidence and circumstances, can fail to acquiesce with us in the opinion of the Justices at Cambridge, who, after *laborious* legal investigation, express their belief in the good motives and honorable conduct of Engine Company No. 13. We think Captain James Quinn entitled to much praise for his prudent and decided conduct at the fire, and also the company under his command for their prompt obedience and orderly conduct on this, as on other occasions."

The report was signed by Engineers William G. Eaton, David Kimball, David Tillson, R. A. Newell, and John Shelton.

FROM JOSEPH L. DREW.

Mr. Joseph L. Drew, of Boston, was an officer of Engine Company No. 13 at the time of the outbreak; went over to Charlestown with the company, and his testimony before the court and jury is copied in a preceding page. Mr. Drew fully agrees with the opinion of Captain Quinn in relation to the inaction and indecision displayed by the Charlestown town authorities, and he expressed the same sentiment to Mr. Austin, while proceeding with the latter from Boston to East Cambridge at the time of the trials, but before he (Mr. Drew) had been called to the stand. The Attorney General asked him what he was to swear to? and Mr. Drew answered, that he should say, if asked, that in his opinion the mob could have been dispersed in the beginning, if there had been prompt and resolute action on the part of the magistrates of the town. A dozen or fifteen good men, of standing and authority, could have prevented the whole great mischief, by warning off the rioters, proclaiming the law, and referring to the consequences of violating it.

CONTEMPORARY DISCUSSION.

Gentlemen who had daughters in the Convent school were subjected to much criticism at the time. Among these were Hon. Samuel P. P. Fay, of Cambridge, Judge of Probate for Middlesex county, and Samuel K. Williams, of Boston, an eminent Counsellor, and a man greatly respected in the community. There were many defamatory and depreciatory reports afloat at the time in regard to the Convent school, some of which reflected severely upon the parents of pupils in the institution. In answer to these, Mr. Williams wrote the following communication to the editor of the Boston Daily Advertiser:—

The interest the public have manifested in regard to the School of the Ursuline Community, whose buildings have, within the last week, been burned to the ground, and the near connection I have had with it for more than three years, renders, I trust, any apology unnecessary for the statement I now make. No request, or intimation even, from any person or persons, has induced or influenced me to make this communication. But I frankly avow that the defamatory and vilely wicked reports which have come to my ears, circulated *insidiously*, and no doubt, by some with great *zeal* and *industry*, have, in my opinion, made it my duty to present myself to the public in a statement of such information as I have in regard to this Institution.

My first acquaintance with this Institution was in the year 1829, and my inquiries were then made to enable me to answer a letter from Mrs. Guisinger, of Philadelphia, the lady of Captain Guisinger, of the United States Navy. In the discharge of my duty on that occasion, I acquired such information as induced me, two years afterwards, to place two of my children at this school, and also the child of a deceased friend, left to my care by the will of her father, and whose mother was also dead. From this time, viz., April, 1831, my acquaintance with the school became very intimate, and my visits to it were, on an average, from that time to the present, once a fortnight.

In December, 1832, the child of my deceased friend became sick, and after remaining at the Institution about two months, was brought to my house, and died there about one month afterwards.

During the sickness of this child, a greater intimacy and a more thorough acquaintance with the inmates of the institution was had, by me and Mrs. W., than had before existed.

In the month of June following the decease of this child, I placed my two younger daughters at this school,— and my four daughters have remained there ever since, except that my eldest has within that time been at home about three months.

The teachers at this school were educated *to teach female youth.* Their early instructions were had with special reference to this, as their *profession* and *duty for life;* and when they have taken their religious vows they are withdrawn from the world, and have dedicated themselves singly to this service and duty.

The school was upon a Catholic foundation, and the teachers were all of a Catholic order of Nuns, viz., of the order of St. Ursuline. The school was, however, in a Protestant community, and more than three fourths of the scholars were of Protestant parents. The school was, therefore, essentially a Protestant school. This will be more readily granted, when it is understood that the teachers have always given the assurance that no formula or catechism should be put into the children's hands except such as the parents should direct; and that in the absence of any direction, the children should be instructed in religious matters only in the broad and clear principles which are to be found in the precepts and examples of our Saviour, without any sectarian bias whatever. This pledge has been always most faithfully redeemed in regard to my children; and I believe it has been equally so in regard to all other children of Protestant parents.

The teachers have paid unwearied attention to the tempers and manners of the children. Their conduct on this most delicate and difficult of subjects has met with my entire satisfaction.

The principles of moral right appear ever to have been kept in steady view.

The health of my children while at the school has been always good. The child under my care, who was taken sick at the school and died at my house, died of consumption, as did also her parents. The attention to her while sick at the school was everything that could be done. Parents, I think, would not have done more.

The progress of my children in their studies, and in the ornamental exercises, has been to my satisfaction. There has been no want of diligence or fidelity on the part of their teachers.

To all the vile surmises, and rumors, and reports which have been put forth to the public, I can only say, that it has appeared to me that as fast and as often as one is met and put down, another has been ushered off to take its place. In regard to the past, the present, and the future, therefore, I have but one observation to make, one opinion to offer, and it is this : —

If there is purity of life to be found by the fireside, or in the families of any of our distinguished Protestant clergymen throughout New England, it in no way surpasses that of these excellent women Sisters of the order of St. Ursuline.

I have here presented a view of my means and opportunities of obtaining information, together with such information as I thought of most interest at this time; and my object has been to disabuse the public of the errors which have acquired currency in the community.

I add herewith for publication the prospectus of the school which was put into my hands in the spring of 1831. The school had existed essentially the same as this prospectus presents up to the time its buildings were wantonly destroyed by an infuriated mob. This prospectus is now no other wise important than as showing what this school promised, and what all who knew it well, knew that it was.

SAMUEL K. WILLIAMS.

URSULINE COMMUNITY, MOUNT BENEDICT, CHARLESTOWN, MASS.

This beautiful and extensive establishment is situated about two and a half miles from Boston, upon a delightful and healthy spot, commanding one of the most beautiful prospects in the United States. In it young ladies are received from the age of six to that of fourteen.

The plan of education pursued by the Ladies of this Community is extensive; comprehending all those attainments which may be found necessary, useful, and ornamental in society. Devoted by their Institute, to the education of female youth, they spare no pains to adorn their minds with useful knowledge, and to form their hearts to virtue.

To attain this twofold object, their first care is to instruct them in the great and sublime truths of religion; to endeavor to impress them with its salutary maxims; and to point out the duties it imposes on them towards their God, their parents, and superiors, towards other members of society, and towards themselves.

The school consists of two *Departments*, distinguished by the appellations of *Senior* and *Junior Class*, each occupying separate apartments, and having no communication whatever.

The young ladies in the Junior Department are taught the common branches of education, such as Reading, Writing, Grammar, Arithmetic, Geography, History, ancient and modern; and particular attention is paid to Orthography. They are also taught all kinds of plain and fancy Needlework, and the *Extra Branches*, if required. When sufficiently advanced, they are removed to the *Senior Department*.

Here are taught plain and ornamental Writing; Composition, both in prose and poetry; ancient, modern, and natural History; Chronology; Mythology;

the use of the Globes; Astronomy; Rhetoric; Logic; Natural and Moral Philosophy; Chemistry; Arithmetic; Geometry; and Botany; every kind of useful and ornamental Needlework; Japanning; Drawing, in all its varieties; Painting in Oil Colors; also, Painting on Velvet, Satin, and Wood; and the beautiful style of Mezzotinto and Poonah Painting. Music, on different instruments, is likewise taught.

The young ladies in this Department may also attend to cookery during the last quarter of their residence in the Institute. They will possess every advantage in this respect, being superintended by a person, who, to a perfect knowledge of the art, has joined many years' experience. The charge is twenty dollars.

To accelerate the advancement of the young ladies in their respective classes, every means is resorted to, which is calculated to act upon the youthful mind, in order to excite, and maintain therein, a laudable emulation; such as, distinction of places; daily marks; weekly repetitions; privileges granted to application and merit; honorable mention, made every month, of those whose assiduity in their studies, and excellency in good conduct, deserve approbation; premiums distributed at the end of the year, &c.

The annual examination takes place in the month of June, commencing on the 29th, and continuing three days. At the close two young ladies are crowned, one in the *Senior*, and the other in the *Junior Class*; the former receiving at the same time a gold medal, and the latter a silver one. These young ladies shall have been in the Institution one year at least; during which time they must have distinguished themselves, by their amiable deportment, general good conduct, and excellence in their studies.

The ladies who preside over this establishment are scrupulously careful to supply those placed under their care with abundant and wholesome food; and to watch over their health as well as their morals, with all the solicitude of maternal tenderness. Cleanliness and neatness are rigorously attended to.

The garden adjoining the establishment, to which the young ladies always have access during the hours of relaxation, is beautifully laid out, and consists of two acres of land. Besides this, they are allowed, on days of recreation, to extend their walks over the whole farm, which embraces twenty-seven acres; always under the immediate superintendence of one or more of the ladies. During the summer season they are allowed two acres of land, which are divided into flower gardens, and are cultivated by themselves.

Parents being ever sensible to the happiness and welfare of their children, and anxious to know even the smallest details of what concerns them, every three months bulletins will be issued relating to their health, the extent of their application, and their progress in study. Care will be likewise taken that their children write to them the 15th of each month.

Three months' notice of the removal of each young lady is requested. No boarder is allowed to sleep out, except in case of illness. Permission to dine out is granted once a month. No visitors are allowed on Sundays. The religious opinions of the children are not interfered with. A vacation of six weeks is allowed every year, commencing on the 1st of July, and terminating on the 15th of August.

The Boston "Recorder," the organ of the Orthodox Congregationalists, had the following, in response to Mr. Williams: —

THE CONVENT. *Religious Instruction.* — Mr. Samuel K. Williams, of this city, who had four daughters in the Convent at Charlestown, has published a statement in the Daily Advertiser, containing the following paragraph.

[Then follows a quotation from the foregoing letter of Mr. Williams, beginning, "The school was upon a Catholic foundation," and ending, " and I believe it has been equally so in regard to all other children of Protestant parents."]

This statement appears to us, and to some other persons, extremely vague and unsatisfactory. Will Mr. Williams answer the following questions?

Had the pupils in the Convent, *Bibles* in their possession, in any language which they could easily read and understand? If so, in what language, and what translation? If they had none, why had they not? If they had, were they permitted to use them at their own discretion? If there were any restrictions upon their use of the Bible, what were they? Did the pupils, while there, use Catholic forms of worship? In what ceremonies, or forms of worship, not in general use among Protestants, did they bear a part? If in any, was it *required* of them? If not, how were they induced to do it?

These questions are suggested by information, apparently worthy of credit, concerning other Convents. We will gladly insert in our paper definite answers to these questions from Mr. Williams, or from any other person, who will give definite answers, and be responsible for them.

Mr. Williams replied in the following letter: —

TO THE EDITOR OF THE BOSTON RECORDER.

I answer the questions you propose in the Recorder, of the 5th inst.

Every pupil at the Convent school was *required* to have a Bible, or at least that part of it called the New Testament. Each of my children had one or the other of these books in the *common English translation*, and the same they had used at the Protestant schools in the city before going to the Convent school; and these books they were not only permitted to read at pleasure, but were *required* to read them on the Sabbath.

It was also made known to me, at the time I first put my children at this school, that if I would furnish them with any book or books of prayers, the teachers would take charge of them so far as to have such book or books of prayers read and studied by my children. And I did accordingly furnish my children with the book of prayers published by the Rev. Mr. Brooks, of Hingham, and with the prayers used at the Stone Chapel in this city. And I have reason to be satisfied with the use my children made of these books while at this school, and *know* that it was a matter of gratification to the teachers that these books were furnished.

The Protestant children had prayers daily by themselves,

morning and night, the children in turn reading the prayers in the order designated by the teachers. I send you herewith copies of the prayers which were thus read. At noon the children together repeated the Lord's Prayer.

All the children attended mass in the chapel on the Sabbath. This was the only Catholic service the Protestant children were *required* to attend. This service was in the Latin language. And my children, and all other Protestant children, were not only allowed, but were required, in attending this service, to have with them either such prayer book as had been furnished them by their parents, or their Bible or Testament, and to employ their minds in reading the same.

In no other ceremonies, or forms of worship, not in general use among Protestants, did the Protestant children at this school bear a part, nor was it required of them to do so.

It has been intimated in some one of the papers of the city, that the children were not allowed to pass the Sabbath out of the school; that they were all required to cross themselves, and that they were aso required to read the Scriptures from a *Catholic Bible.* To the two last intimations I state, that it is not true that my children, or that any Protestant children have ever been *required* to cross themselves at any time, or on any occasion, while at this school. Nor have they ever been *required*, or even allowed, to read from a Catholic Bible.

In regard to passing the Sabbath out of the school, I can only say, that my children passed the Sabbath with me as often as I asked to have them, which was about every fourth Sabbath in the year. SAMUEL K. WILLIAMS.

MORNING PRAYERS.

Most holy and adorable Trinity, one God in three persons, I believe that thou art here present; I adore thee with the most profound humility; I desire, in the sincerity of my heart, to praise and glorify thee now and forever.

I give thee thanks, O Lord, from the bottom of my heart, for all the favors I have received from thee. It is thy loving goodness which has brought me safe to the beginning of this day. I mean, with the help of thy grace, to serve and honor thee, during the whole course of it. I offer up to thee all my thoughts, words, and actions. Give them thy blessing, that they may all be animated with thy love, and tend to thy greater glory.

Adorable Jesus! divine Model of that perfection to which we should all aspire, I will endeavor, this day, to follow thy example; to be mild, humble, chaste, zealous, patient, and charitable like thee. I will be particularly attentive not to relapse this day into those sins I have so often committed, but to guard against them, with thy gracious assistance.

Thou knowest, O Lord, my weakness. I can do nothing without the help of thy grace. Do not refuse, O merciful Lord, to bestow it on me, according to my wants. Give me strength, that I may avoid the evil thou forbiddest, practise the good thou commandest, cheerfully bear whatever trials and crosses thou shalt be pleased to send upon me.

Here they recited the Lord's Prayer.

HYMN.

The rising sun now brings the day,
And drives the shades of night away;
Eternal Light, O God, inspire,
With heavenly songs, our morning choir.

Let our first voices sound thy name,
Thy love, our first desires inflame,
That all our following actions may
By thee be sanctified to-day.

So rule our minds that they may be
The unspotted seat of chastity;
Shut out all access by which the eyes
Let in deceit and vanities.

O God of peace, our tongues restrain,
That we from quarrels may refrain,
From slander let our speech be free;
Let's live in peace and charity.

This prayer, most gracious Father, hear;
Thy equal Son incline his ear,
Who with the Holy Ghost and thee,
Doth live and reign eternally.

EVENING PRAYERS.

I adore thee, O my God, and most humbly acknowledging my unworthiness, in the presence of thy eternal Majesty. I believe in thee, because thou art Truth itself; I hope in thee, because thou art faithful to thy word; I love thee with my whole heart, because thou art infinitely amiable; and, for thy sake, I love my neighbor as myself.

How shall I be able to thank thee, O Lord, for all thy favors? Thou hast thought of me from all eternity; thou hast brought me forth from nothing; thou hast given thy life to redeem me; and thou continuest still, daily to load me with thy favors.

Alas! my God, what return can I make thee for all thy benefits, and in particular, for the favors of this day? Join me, ye blessed spirits, and all ye saints, in praising the God of mercies, who is so bountiful to so unworthy a creature.

O Holy Ghost, eternal source of light, remove the darkness which hides from me the number and grievousness of my offences. Show me, I beseech thee, the sins I have this day committed, in thought, word and action. Give me a feeling sense of them, that I may detest them from my heart, and dread nothing so much, as ever to commit them again.

Here they said the Lord's Prayer.

HYMN.

Before the closing of the day,
Creator, thee we humbly pray
That, for thy wonted mercy's sake,
Thou us into protection take.

May nothing in our minds excite
Vain dreams and phantoms of the night;
Our enemies repress, that so
Our bodies no uncleanness know.

To Jesus, from a Virgin sprung,
Be glory given, and praises sung;
The same to God the Father be,
And Holy Ghost eternally.

On the 25th of September, 1834, Judge Fay sent the following communication to the Boston Daily Advertiser:—

MR. HALE: The subjoined letter was received by me some time since, in answer to one, in which I requested from the writer such information as her long residence in the Ursuline Convent at Charlestown would enable her to furnish respecting the rules and practices of that Community; particularly as to their treatment of the sick, and as to improper restraints on the liberty of the inmates. This request was made in consequence of finding, in the course of my inquiries into the causes of the destruction of the Nunnery, that among the stories in circulation affecting its character, and which had excited the popular fury against it, one charged them with the grossest inhumanity to the sick, in the last stages of life, and particularly to a Mrs. Mary Magdalen, who died in the latter part of 1831; and another imputed to the Superior of the Community the most unjustifiable restraints upon the personal liberty of the inmates. I also thought that Miss Alden (who is personally a stranger to me, but who, as I learn from others, is of the most respectable character and standing in society), was a person whose former acquaintance with the Convent, and whose present removal from it would render her testimony peculiarly valuable to those persons who are desirous to know the truth, and who are not too prejudiced to see and acknowledge it. The letter was enclosed to me by Hiram O. Alden, Esq., postmaster at Belfast, brother of the writer, who is undoubtedly well known to many in this city and vicinity. He stated that he had perused his sister's letter, and assures me that its representations are such as he has always heard from her, and that he had determined to send his own daughter to the Ursuline Convent for her education as soon as she was of suitable age. He is a Protestant. I believe Miss Alden's letter will serve to disabuse the community at large of many errors and prejudices created by the foulest calumnies, and I trust that you and other editors of papers, who are desirous that truth should prevail, and that justice may be done to the much injured Ursulines, will publish it. I have her authority to make such use of it as I may deem expedient to promote these good ends.

Your obedient servant,
SAMUEL P. P. FAY.

Then follows the letter of Miss Alden, thus:—

BELFAST, Sept. 4, 1834.

SIR: I have received your letter, and hasten to give you an early answer. The task is not a pleasant one under such circumstances. No delicacy of feeling, however, shall withhold me from doing justice, as far as lies in my power, to that estimable and never-to-be-forgotten Community.

In the month of December, 1827, I entered the Ursuline Convent, Mount Benedict, as a candidate for that Community. After remaining about two years, I became convinced that I had no vocation for that state of life. Having become exceedingly attached to the Lady Superior, and those of her Community, I felt an unwillingness to leave. I found, however, that it was vain to think of compelling myself to remain, and I immediately made known my feelings on the subject to the Lady Superior. So far from meeting with the least opposition, she replied, that "strongly as she was attached, and dearly as she loved me, she must advise me to go, if I saw that I could not be happy there;" for, she continued, "no one can judge of that so well as yourself, and it shall be left to your own decision;" telling me, at the same time, that "their Rules and Constitution did not allow any one to remain but such as found their happiness there, and *there* only." She told me that I was at liberty to go, whenever I pleased, and should be provided with every thing requisite for my departure, which was done *two years* after; having remained there that length of time, merely from personal attachment to the Lady Superior, and her no less worthy Community. During my residence there (a period of four years), I can truly say that I never saw *one* action to censure.

Their character is as unimpeachable as their conduct is pure and blameless. I can assure you, that as they appear at the parlor, so are they in their most unguarded moments — no unbending from that sweetness and affability of manner which characterize them all. Every duty, both temporal and spiritual, is discharged with the greatest fidelity. The love of God, and the hope of heaven, is the motive for every action. As teachers, nothing can exceed the care, attention, and kindness which is bestowed on *all* placed under their instruction. As persons secluded from the world and devoted to God, their purity of conversation and moral principles, their nobleness of soul, their charity, kindness, and forbearance to each other, cannot fail of being a most edifying example to all around them.

My situation in that Community was such as to render me thoroughly acquainted with every member, and every part of the house. And I solemnly assure you, there was not the least thing existing there, that any person could disapprove, were he ever so prejudiced.

As regards the school, I have ever recommended it to every parent, as the only *secure* place for the education of daughters in New England, or even the United States. I say *secure*, for so I consider it, in respect to the allurements held out to the young mind by a fascinating world, in most of our boarding-schools.

With respect to Mrs. Mary John, I was at the Convent* the day after her return there; I saw her in the parlor; she told me she had been very ill. At that time I knew nothing of her unfortunate departure. I found Dr. Thompson there also, who prohibited my seeing the Superior for the space of five days, in consequence of one of her eyes being dangerously affected. At the expiration of that time I passed the day there. I saw Mrs. Mary John, who related to me the particulars of her going; — said she could not realize that it was so; expressed the greatest horror at having taken such a step; and said that she would prefer death to leaving. She has been in that Community thirteen years, and has had the black veil eleven years. She always appeared perfectly happy, and I have no doubt that she was so, as we have had many conversations on that subject. She has told me repeatedly that she could never cease to be thankful for having been called to that happy state of life. If she had changed her mind, she had only to say so, to be *free*, as I am at present. Never, I can assure you, has there been, or can there be, according to the Rules and Constitutions of the order, any *improper restraints* imposed on any person entering there. While I was a resident there, several left without the least opposition on the part of the Superior, or any other person.

As it respects the sick, nothing, I assure you, can be further from the truth than the assertions of Miss ——. For never, by any person (I will not except my own parents' house), have I received greater kindness, or more attention in sickness, than during my stay in that house.

With the greatest respect, &c.
CAROLINE FRANCES ALDEN.

HON. S. P. P. FAY.

---

* Miss Alden was on a visit to Boston at the time of the conflagration of the Convent.

www.ingramcontent.com/pod-product-compliance
Lightning Source LLC
Chambersburg PA
CBHW021949160426
43195CB00011B/1292